THE POSTCARD HISTORY SERIES

Jersey City
IN VINTAGE POSTCARDS

St. Joseph's Home for the Blind was founded in the 19th century to provide services for the sightless, as did the St. Joseph's School for the Blind. The two organizations published numerous cards picturing their activities. These illustrations educated and built understanding. Today their facility on Pavonia Avenue is a 129-bed nursing home operated by the Sisters of St. Joseph of Peace. It serves both the blind and sighted, with a preference for the former. (Collection of Cynthia Harris.)

THE POSTCARD HISTORY SERIES

Jersey City
IN VINTAGE POSTCARDS

Randall Gabrielan

ARCADIA

First printed in 1999.
Reprinted in 2001.

Published by Arcadia Publishing,
an imprint of Tempus Publishing, Inc.
2A Cumberland Street
Charleston, SC 29401

Printed in Great Britain.

For all general information contact Arcadia Publishing at:
Telephone 843-853-2070
Fax 843-853-0044
E-Mail sales@arcadiapublishing.com

For customer service and orders:
Toll-Free 1-888-313-2665

Visit us on the internet at http://www.arcadiapublishing.com

On the Cover: Colgate from the air depicts the vast operation that formerly dominated downtown Jersey City. (Collection of Cynthia Harris.)

This book is dedicated to Rita Murphy, whom I first knew as a teacher at Snyder High School. It was an unexpected pleasure to discover some years later that this popular and effective member of the history department, then a fellow shore resident, remembered a former student, shared an affinity of interests, and provided encouragement with the same cheer and charm that endeared her to so many at Snyder.

CONTENTS

INTRODUCTION

The picture postcard began as a postal experiment in the late 19th century and became a worldwide collecting mania early in the 20th century. A frenzied interest in postcards reached its peak in the years between 1905 and 1915, a period roughly coinciding with Jersey City's rise as a transportation, business, and population center. Major postcard companies published a profusion of Jersey City images then, but it was also a time when manufacturing and distribution systems enabled even small stores to become postcard publishers, too.

The scenes in this book are thus skewed to that period, known in the trade as the "postcard era," or the so-called "golden age of postcards." It was a great time for Jersey City, one when the Board of Trade could unabashedly claim the following when measuring 20 years' progress in its 1910 *Jersey City of Today*, now a classic work of Jersey City history and biography:

> The Jersey City of twenty years ago is in nowise the Jersey City of to-day. This is a new city you are walking in, alive, tensely alive to all that is going on about it and standing at the threshold of the West receiving and discharging the richest cargoes of America's great domain; progressive even to the smallest street urchin who sells you your evening paper and alert to all the possibilities of its wonderful location.

That author's enthusiastic extrapolation of trends in the city's growing population projected a Jersey City with over a million residents by 1936!

The author dislikes the "golden age" term, as it discourages interest in the on-going development of the postcard as a communication and advertising medium. However, the reality of the distribution of postcard images is such that well-known places extant around 1910 may exist in multiple fine examples, while places of equal or greater importance dating after 1915 may not exist on a card or may have been published only on inferior examples. Familiarity with postcard periods is helpful for understanding this work, which makes reference to the terms.

The Private Mailing Card Era
Postcard use began as a practical matter after the Private Mailing Card Act of 1898, which effectively standardized postcard appearance. Private Mailing Card era postcards were typically imprinted on the back or address side, with the slogan, "Private Mailing Card—Authorized by Act of Congress, May 19, 1898." Jersey City examples are few.

The Postcard Era
Foreign manufacturers dominated the 1905–1915 period, especially the Germans, whose lithography process produced most of the better cards. Photographers printed actual photographs on postcard size printing paper, typically with the words "Post Card" printed on the back. This period is divided by legislation, effective March 1, 1907, that permitted the writing of messages on the back, which had theretofore been reserved for the address. Their distinguishing mark is a vertical line in the middle of the address side, dividing the era into "undivided" and "divided back" periods. High protective tariffs began in 1909 that steered the market towards inferior American-made cards, the waning of interest that follows any over-heated collecting mania (Beanie Baby buffs beware), and the onset of World War I brought the period to a close.

The White Border Era
This period, loosely defined as 1915 to 1930, is characterized by its often dismal, poorly printed cards surrounded by a border of white space on all sides. Its inferior graphics represent the low point of postcard production, with the period's only redeeming virtue being the realization that important places built in this period are often known only on white-border cards.

The Linen Era
A new printing process prevailed in the period c. 1930 to 1950, one that permitted bright colors on an absorbent, rough-surfaced stock that had a look and feel characteristic of linen. A lack of clarity lessened their collector appeal, but the interest in linens has risen recently with their aging. An appreciation has developed for their frequently outlandish colors, as well as the travel and advertising topics popular in the linen era.

Chromes and the Modern Era
Printed color cards, often with the clarity of photographs, were introduced nationally c. 1940, but few Jersey City examples exist from that decade. Their size varies from the standard 3 1/2 by 5 1/2 inches to the current Continental format, approximately 4 1/4 by 5 3/4 inches, the latter being long-popular in Europe. Photographs were issued on postcard paper past 1915, and various other processes were introduced that did not fit the widely accepted postcard categories.

The issuers of Jersey City postcards, as well as those who stayed out of this market, are also a subject worthy of study. Raphael Tuck & Son and Detroit Publishing Company apparently avoided Jersey City, while the Illustrated Post Card Company had only a few examples. A British firm, Valentine and Sons, made a major commitment in Jersey City with a long series of numbered color view cards. Their six-digit numbers, typically beginning with 2 or 4 and accompanied by the initials "JV," are recognizable in their reproductions herein. The firm's decline is characteristic of one reaction to the protective tariffs. They took an American partner, the Hugh C. Leighton Company, and the new firm's product often showed a significant decrease in quality.

Jersey City had a number of local publishers that printed numerous examples of postcards. The J.C. Voigt Company issued an incredibly long-numbered series of German-printed cards, most in a gray monochrome. Their numbers reached over 600. However, their total output is unclear because the absence of a list makes it uncertain if their numbers are consecutive or skipped. The process for a small business to send pictures overseas for postcard production was simple. The practice became popular with pharmacies, which typically produced cards of their own stores. Major markets often had a photographer publish actual photographs as postcards. Jersey City's practitioner, Charles Lefferts, produced outstanding examples. Manhattan Post Card Company, although not producing cards until c. the late 1920s, had perhaps the longest career publishing Jersey City cards. Regrettably, they were not able to be located recently.

Various other methods and types of publication have been employed, matters beyond the scope of these brief remarks. Offset printing has been utilized only infrequently, but is perhaps a method that can address the high cost of commercial chrome production. An excellent essay, suitable for such printing, is on page 47. The predilection for older cards will usually satisfy most collectors, but the author believes the postcard should be viewed as a continuous process rather than as an object of nostalgia and hopes that growing interest in the older cards will stimulate new card publication.

The book is organized geographically into a minimal number of broadly defined sections, with a preference to current name usage over historical names. It is conceded that geographical differences may arise with overlapping or imprecise sectional boundaries.

The author typically ends one work preparing for a follow-up. Although a second volume can not be assured, access to additional images for possible future use is welcome. His address and number are 71 Fish Hawk Drive, Middletown, New Jersey, 07748, (732) 671-2645.

Acknowledgments

Cynthia Harris supported this project with an incomparable act of generosity that significantly enhanced the quality of the book. She gave encouragement and offered liberal access to her superlative collection. These deeds asserted her pride in our old home town and that collection, and showed that the postcards are more meaningful when shared with the public and given to foster a better appreciation of Jersey City.

John Rhody's help has been regular, frequent, and of outstanding quality for most of the author's Monmouth County titles. He led this project with many fine images, with a number unused and ready for inclusion in a second work.

Thanks to the Jersey City Public Library, particularly Kenneth French, librarian of their New Jersey Room and fellow Arcadia author, for access to their postcard collection and for assistance with reference materials.

Thanks to all the lenders, including Steven Cohen, Moe Cuocci, Gary Dubnik, Mary Ann Smith Jerez, Richard La Rovere, Rita Murphy, Suzanne Parmly, Special Collections and Archives, Rutgers University Libraries, Harold Solomon, and Marion Wardell, as their collective efforts made this book possible.

Forrest S. Smith, born 1904 and raised on Bentley Avenue, became senior partner of the Jersey City law firm of Smith, James & Mathias. He demonstrated c. 1914 that reindeer were not the only animals helping Santa.

One

DOWNTOWN

FROM PAULUS HOOK TO PAVONIA

Paulus Hook's Monument, Paulus Hook Square, Jersey City, N. J.

Paulus Hook, once an island about east of Van Vorst Street and one of the earliest settlements in the future Jersey City, was captured by the British early in the Revolutionary War. It was the site of a bold attempt by colonial forces to capture their fort in August 1779. They took a number of prisoners, so the clash is regarded as a great victory. It was commemorated by this battle monument which stood in the intersection of Washington and Grand Streets until falling after being repeatedly struck by trucks. A modern replacement, an obelisk, was erected in a park on the southeast corner. This view looks west on Grand. The structure on the north side with the pyramidal roof is now the Humanities Building of St. Peter's Preparatory School.

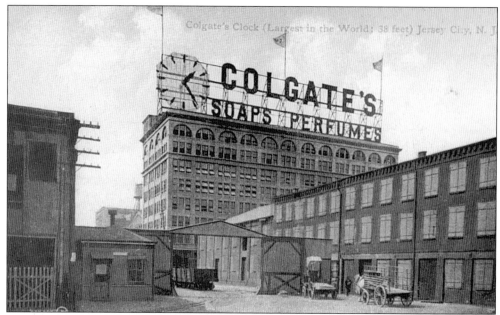

The Colgate Company, manufacturers of soaps and perfumes, moved from New York to Jersey City in 1847. In time, the company covered several blocks, focusing on Hudson and Grand Streets where they had dozens of buildings, as depicted on the cover. Their erection of "the world's largest clock" (as measured by the face) gained wide-spread recognition for their Jersey City operation. The precise date of the mounting of the first clock is lost, but it was probably c. 1908, around the time this eight-story concrete building was completed. A new and slightly larger clock was mounted in 1924, built to eliminate a challenge to the "largest" claim. This building, seen c. 1910, was demolished in the 1980s for construction of the office now on the site. (Collection of Cynthia Harris.)

The clock, having become one of Jersey City's most recognizable symbols, was remounted on the riverfront where it remains today. The letters and advertising message have varied over the years and are now styled to resemble one of Colgate's best-known products, the toothpaste tube. This image is a modern photograph printed on postcard stock. John Kowalak of River Edge, New Jersey, has been custom-making postcards for many years, meeting collector demand and continuing the photographic postcard tradition. After all, for some, the postcard back can be as important as the illustration. (Collection of Cynthia Harris.)

The Jersey City Post Office, founded in 1807, needed expanded facilities in the 1870s, but could not secure funding for a modern building. The handsome Italianate Dudley Gregory house at the northwest corner of Sussex and Washington Streets was purchased and expanded by the one-story structure at right. It was replaced by the building at bottom, with the former post office corner now the site of Public School 16.

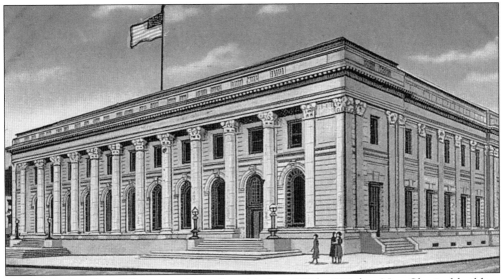

The Jersey City Post Office was relocated in this fine, 200-by-220-foot Neo-Classical building located on the Washington Street block between Montgomery and York Streets. The building, clad in Mount Waldo granite and designed by the supervising architect of the Treasury Department, had its cornerstone laid on June 11, 1912, and was dedicated on November 7, 1913. The post office is a neighborhood rarity, a little-changed building still functioning for its original use. This image is a white border card dating to c. 1920s.

St. Peter's Church was organized in 1831. Their first church building, located on Grand Street, opened in 1837 and was consecrated by Archbishop Hughes of New York in 1839. The edifice pictured on this *c.* 1908 postcard, completed in the latter 1860s at the northeast corner of Grand and Van Vorst Streets, was transferred to the Jesuits *c.* 1897 as an inducement to found a Catholic college. The building, having sustained damage, was closed as unsafe on December 15, 1957, and was demolished in the summer of 1958. It was replaced by the present church in 1961. (Special Collections & Archives, Rutgers University Libraries.)

St. Peter's College, chartered in 1872, began its building program in 1877, erecting this Beaux Arts classroom building on Grand Street, behind the church located on the northeast corner of Van Vorst Street. (Collection of Cynthia Harris.)

St. Aloysius Academy was founded by the Sisters of Charity on York Street in 1865. They were given the first St. Peter's Church at Grand Street in 1888, which served as a school prior to the erection of this fine Romanesque-style building at 110 Grand Street. The cornerstone was laid in 1889, while the school was completed for the September 1891 academic year. Growth of the student body caused the school to divide its operation into three locations. The three parts rejoined in 1928 at a new building at Hudson (Kennedy) Boulevard and Kensington Avenue. (Collection Jersey City Public Library.)

A fire on Pier B caused extensive damage March 19, 1909, which threatened to close shipping into the river. The fire, which smouldered long after it was controlled, was extinguished through the help of New York City fire boats. The perspective of the photographer was probably a tall building in lower Manhattan. (Courtesy of Moe Cuocci.)

Two *c.* 1890s Romanesque-style bank buildings are pictured here on the west side of Washington Street. The Hudson County National Bank at right, on the corner of York Street, no longer stands (The site is a parking lot.), but the People's Savings Bank building is still occupied by its successor organization, the Provident Institution for Savings. The card is dated *c.* 1905.

The former Union Trust Company Building, erected *c.* 1910 on the southwest corner of Montgomery and Washington Streets, still stands and is recognizable, although it has changed grade-floor windows. The tall building to its right is the New Jersey Title & Guarantee Trust Company's 1890 office. One of the city's most striking business buildings, it was remodeled for housing.

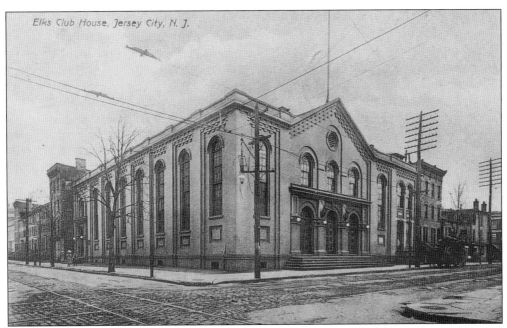

Elks Club House, Jersey City, N. J.

The c. 1890s Elks Hall stood on the corner of York and Henderson Streets until an unspecified date. (Collection of Cynthia Harris.)

Rudermond Industrial had an extensive yard at the foot of Henderson Street on the old Morris Canal basin. They had six floating dry docks and a crane with a 120-ton capacity and specialized in the tugs, barges, and offshore supply vessels that once were so active in local water. This is a chrome advertising card, perhaps from the 1960s.

Exchange Place was once a rail hub as the eastern terminus of the Pennsylvania Railroad, where New York-bound passengers exchanged a train seat for a place on a ferryboat. It was also the origin of most Jersey City trolley lines. The terminal pictured on this c. 1907 card was built in 1899, having replaced the 1891 terminal destroyed by fire in 1898. The terminal was demolished in the early 1960s. Its former site is now the park built on a pier, named for former Jersey City historian J. Owen Grundy.

The north side of Montgomery Street at Exchange Place is seen here c. 1910, with the older Pennsylvania Railroad office at left. They built the one on the right in 1901, a building demolished c. 1960s. The site was a parking lot for many years prior to the construction of Exchange Place Centre, seen on the top of the next page in the 1980s. (Collection of Cynthia Harris.)

Tall office towers characterize the new Jersey City, becoming as prevalent as railroad terminals were in the old City. The 495-foot Exchange Place Centre, which is seen at the right, was designed by Harry B. Mahler of the Grad Partnership, Newark, and was the tallest building in New Jersey when completed in 1988. That distinction now belongs to the 550-foot 101 Hudson Street, which was designed by Brennan Beer German, architects of New York, and was completed in 1991. It is the focal point of the redevelopment of the Colgate site. The First National Bank Building at far left, built in 1920 and designed by Alfred Bossom, was gutted in its remodeling as modern offices. The camera's perspective from J. Owen Grundy Park distorts the height of the tall buildings in relation to one another.

Exchange Place, Jersey City

The Lincoln Trust Company Building, seen on a c. 1905 card, once stood on the northwest corner of Montgomery and Washington Streets. Paulus Hook Tower now fills that block west to Warren Street. (Collection of Cynthia Harris.)

In this *c.* 1905 card, the trolley, heading east on Montgomery Street to the "New York Ferry," is about to pass number 68, the site of the Grand Hotel (one of many in Jersey City at the time), and Dr. John Van Nostrand's dental office. The high rise tower of Battery View is now on that corner, the northeast one with Washington Street. The Lincoln Trust Company Building is on the west side of the intersection. (Collection of Cynthia Harris.)

The south side of Montgomery Street is seen in a second view, *c.* 1910, of the intersection with Washington. This early-city automobile driver was substantially out-numbered by four-legged transport. (Collection of Cynthia Harris.)

Jersey City's Beaux Arts City Hall, designed by Hugh Roberts in conjunction with Detwiller & Melendy of New York (*American Architect* April 20, 1893), faces Grove Street, occupying the block surrounded by Mercer (at left), Henderson, and Montgomery Streets. The building, completed in 1896, lost its cupolas in the mid-1950s and had its fourth floor gutted by fire in 1979, but it was handsomely restored (without the cupolas). The Philip Martiny Soldiers and Sailors Monument, dedicated Memorial Day, 1899, is visible in front on this *c.* 1906 Lefferts photographic card. (Collection Jersey City Public Library.)

The L-shaped Majestic Theater was the main structure on the northwest corner of Grove (front) and Montgomery Streets until demolished in the recent past. Actually, the facade of the *c.* 1900 building remains, with hopes raised for a new theater, which would incorporate the facade. The corner building remains open, while the one at right is boarded-up. The pictured scene faces city hall. (Collection of Cynthia Harris.)

Was that face in the facade, to the right of the light, keeping watch over the southeast corner of Montgomery and Monmouth Streets? Charles J. McCloskey published this card of his pharmacy, c. 1910. New housing is on the site. McCloskey had a second store on Washington Street. (Collection of Cynthia Harris.)

Montgomery Street is seen here c. 1910 looking east at the intersection of Jersey Avenue, with a corner of the Jersey City Public Library at left. Van Vorst Park is at right, recalling the name of Cornelius Van Vorst and Van Vorst Township, a separate municipality from 1841 until its annexation by Jersey City ten years later. The park is surrounded by many Italianate-brownstone buildings that make-up the core of the National Register Van Vorst Park Historic District. (Collection of Cynthia Harris.)

St. Bridget's Roman Catholic Church was founded in 1869, with the construction of a small-frame church building. This large Gothic edifice was erected in the 1880s on the northeast corner of Montgomery and Brunswick Streets and was designed by Patrick C. Keely of Brooklyn, the major area Catholic architect of the latter 19th century. The church is one of five joined in 1998 as the Parish of the Resurrection (see page 31), which is evaluating facility needs at publication time. This church is little changed, although the rose window has been replaced by a smaller one, and other windows have been bricked in. (Collection Jersey City Public Library.)

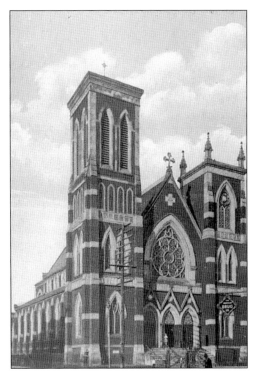

The northwest corner of Jersey Avenue (right) and Bright Street is in reasonably bright condition, nine decades after the publication of this c. 1910 card. The Knights of Columbus Hall on the corner (today missing the top of its tower) is now the First Christian Pentecostal Academy (with bookstore). St. Mark's at right is now the Bethel Baptist Church. The other buildings have survived, although some are missing their decorative features. (Collection of Cynthia Harris.)

On the right of this view of Mercer Street, looking west from Barrow Street, ten c. 1870 Italianate-style, limestone-clad rowhouses are pictured that have been given the separate street designation of Paulmier Place. Paulmier is believed to be the surname of the architect that designed the houses, a story regularly repeated and commonly accepted. However, a diligent search has not found a Paulmier, let alone reference to this work. The architect and builder deserve to be remembered, as the row is quite striking, with most houses restored or refurbished over the recent past. (Collection of Cynthia Harris.)

Mercer east of Barrow has not fared as well as the block at top. The building on the right is gone, but most of the street is intact, although the brick facing of some structures leaves something to be desired. City hall (see page 19) is visible in the background. Both scenes were photographed the same summer afternoon around 1910. (Collection of Cynthia Harris.)

Two substantial Greek-Revival houses with Ionic capitals on their porticos were built on the south side of Wayne Street c. 1840. The one pictured, Cornelius Van Vorst's, was demolished c. 1930, replaced by the brick apartment now on the site. The second, built for Dr. William Barrow, stands east of the St. Matthew's Evangelical Lutheran Church (built 1898), which owns and is restoring the house as a community historical and cultural resource. Most of the street is well preserved, although at left, the first building off the corner has been replaced by number 100 Wayne. (Collection of Jersey City Public Library.)

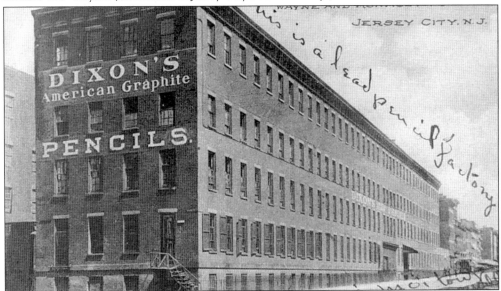

The Joseph Dixon Crucible Company was founded in Salem, Massachusetts, in 1827, and moved to Jersey City not long after. They were manufacturers of a full line of graphite products with their best-known product being the "Ticonderoga" brand pencil. This building facing Monmouth Street is one of a large complex that was remodeled for housing in the 1980s, a complex now known as Dixon Mills. The building is in well-preserved condition. Even the exterior staircase is in place. A stem of Wayne Street, on the site, is closed to traffic. (Collection of Cynthia Harris.)

The C. Martens Company had an enormous bakery at Mercer, Wayne, and Fremont Streets and claimed to turn out 50,000 loaves a day around 1910. They obviously needed quite a few delivery wagons, with the location of this line-up, seen on a photographic card, not specified. (Collection of Cynthia Harris.)

The Old Stone House, a tavern at the southeast corner of Grove Street and Newark Avenue, had the stature of at least a minor landmark, but there is no known record of its origin or demise. It may have dated from the first half of the 19th century and was likely demolished in the 1930s. The Fitzgerald-Holota Park is on the site now. (Collection of Cynthia Harris.)

Newark Avenue once began at Montgomery Street, the streets pictured here, c. 1907. Don't look for this intersection today. It is not a matter of its being unrecognizable. It's gone! The work of 1950s urban renewal obliterated it and paved it over for the site of the Gregory Apartments. It is Montgomery Street, as the tower of city hall in the left background demonstrates that. (Collection of Cynthia Harris.)

The street outside the Grove Street PATH (Tubes) station is now characterized by a large office tower and a collection of older buildings and vacant lots, obscuring the perspective of this c. 1905 card.

The Newark Avenue scene at Erie Street *c.* 1910 had two street clocks. One still stands at left, then the shop of C.G. Rochat & Sons. The curve in the background was at Grove Street. (Collection of Cynthia Harris.)

The handsome row of commercial Italianate buildings on the left probably originated around the 1880s. The former city hall is one building beyond the Baum Bros. sign.

The Bijou was built for dramatic theater, but Keith & Proctor changed it to a vaudeville house *c.* 1907. The building no longer stands. It was replaced by a parking lot. The card is from *c.* 1904.

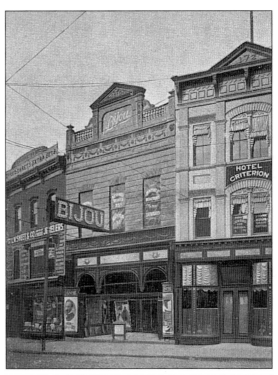

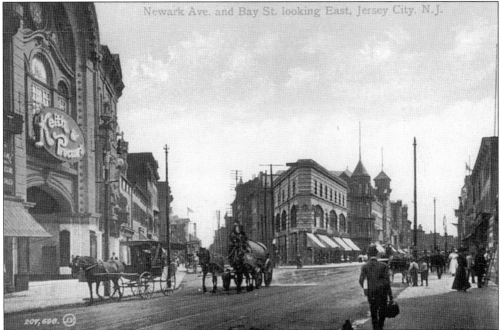

The Keith & Proctor Theater is the former Bijou with a new Beaux Arts facade. The irregular street grid produces a small triangular block with Erie Street, filled by the building at center. The point of the triangle is now marred by a newsstand built into the structure. The conical domed tower is on the Fischer Building, an attractive structure that has seen better days, as its upper stories are now boarded-up. (Collection of Cynthia Harris.)

The solid, Romanesque Revival-style firehouse is a marked contrast to the adjoining stores and apartments. Many multi-alarm Jersey City fires in the early decades of the 20th century were tenement fires.

Few downtown apartments in 1903 had hot running water, so the opening that year of the municipal bathhouse at 9 Coles Street was a major enhancement of public sanitation. The building, designed by John T. Rowland Jr., had a 5,000-square-foot, glazed-brick interior, a frosted skylight, 32 showers and lockers, and a 22-by-80-foot swimming pool holding 65,000 gallons. Bathers and swimmers went through in 20-minute shifts. The week's schedule was organized with different periods for men, women, and children, the latter divided among students and working boys. Strict sanitary rules applied. The city disposed of the then-closed facility in 1964. (Collection of Cynthia Harris.)

This *c.* 1910 view of Jersey Avenue looking south is dominated by the North Baptist Church on the northeast corner of Fourth Street. Most of the street is intact, but the church is missing its steeple and has many windows bricked-in. Its survival, however, is a testament of dedication by those repairing the *c.* 1890 building after it was gutted by fire on October 19, 1978. The congregation is now known as the North Baptist Spanish Church. (Collection of Cynthia Harris.)

Fourth Street east from Coles Street to Jersey Avenue is a well-preserved block, although it seems inevitable one or more re-faced houses will be less than faithful to the original fabric. A later building on Jersey Avenue obscures the present view of the North Baptist Church. (Collection of Cynthia Harris.)

St. Michael's Roman Catholic Church was founded in 1860, inheriting a building from St. Mary's. This 80-by-180-foot Romanesque church, designed by Patrick C. Keely, was begun in 1873, dedicated on October 8, 1876, and built at Ninth and Erie Streets. The interior is richly decorated and is known for its fine acoustics. Today the well-preserved, little-changed St. Michael's is the site of the Vietnamese Apostociate in the Newark Archdiocese. This is a *c.* 1906 card. (Collection of Cynthia Harris.)

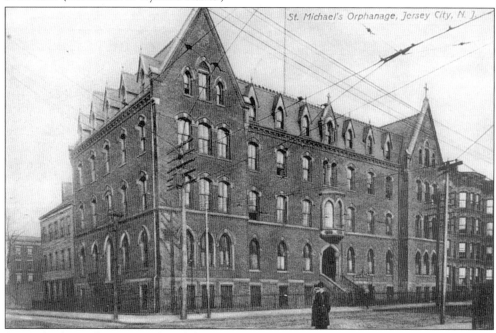

St. Michael's Orphanage was founded in 1876 following the gift of a house, given by parishioner Harold Henwood, which was formerly a private residence and later a children's home. This substantial, new building was erected in 1880 and contained room for the Academy of the Sacred Heart. The orphanage was closed *c.* 1912; the property was acquired in time by the Board of Education of Jersey City, which built Public School 37 on the site. This Voigt 272 card is from about 1909. (Collection of Cynthia Harris.)

The former St. Michael's Orphanage is seen on Pavonia Avenue *c.* 1906. The Roman Catholic Parish of the Resurrection was formed July 1, 1997, by the joining of five downtown Jersey City churches. They are St. Boniface, St. Bridget's, St. Mary's, St. Michael's, and St. Peter's. (Collection of Cynthia Harris.)

St. Boniface was organized in 1863 as a parish for Jersey City Germans; its early meetings were held in various rented quarters. The cornerstone of this Gothic church on First Street was laid on May 8, 1865. Mass was first celebrated around July, as the basement was then completed. Mass was moved to the sanctuary in late 1866, and the facade was completed in July 1869. Their school was completed in November 1888. This card, dating *c.* 1906, also shows the rectory. (Collection of Cynthia Harris.)

31

An early effort to dig a tunnel under the Hudson River began in 1874. It was a project fraught with tunneling difficulties, financial problems, long delays, and fatal accidents. Work was dormant for 11 years until William Gibbs McAdoo, a New York lawyer, carried through the earlier project, which he learned about only after envisioning the need for the tunnel. The construction began in 1902, and the tunnel became the road for the Hudson & Manhattan Railroad, which opened in 1908 and was popularly known as "the Tubes." The line would transform settlement patters, expanding residential opportunities for New York workers. Investors are seen on a demonstration run in what was popularly known at the outset as "the McAdoo tunnels." (Collection of Cynthia Harris.)

The Holland Tunnel, a seven-year project of the Port Authority of New York, was, at 8,557 feet, the longest underwater tunnel in the world when completed in 1927. Named for its engineer, Clifford M. Holland, the twin tubes connected Jersey City with Canal Street in New York. The project's greatest challenge was ventilation, the removal of exhaust gases, and the pumping in of fresh air. The innovative system that was developed became a model for tunnel ventilation worldwide. The long-term portent of the tunnels for Jersey City may not have been widely seen at the time. Motor transport would become a cheaper, flexible, dominant means of moving goods, diminishing the significance of the city as a rail center. The card is an early 1960s chrome.

Two

LAFAYETTE

Lafayette Park, built early in this century and dedicated April 25, 1902, is surrounded by Lafayette, Van Horne, and Maple Streets. The *c.* 1908 view looks north, with the bridge at right, the Johnston Avenue crossing of the Morris Canal. (Collection of Cynthia Harris.)

Prescott Street, originating at the northern end, and Randolph Avenue at the south, make the crossing of the major thoroughfares of Grand and Communipaw Avenues, with the meeting of Garfield Avenue a seven-street juncture. The "junction" name originated from the late-19th-century crossing of several trolley lines. Several missing buildings and a decline in commercial activity mar the present scene, but the side avenues still suggest its importance as a transportation hub. (Collection of Cynthia Harris.)

Frank O. Cole's pharmacy is seen *c.* 1909 at the southwest corner of Grand and Summit Avenues. A Cole pharmacy is still at the location, although the storefront has been changed considerably. (Collection of Cynthia Harris.)

34

The G. Dewey Cummings Sunoco station held a heavily trafficked corner at 470 Communipaw Avenue. The site is still occupied by Sunoco, but the surroundings have changed. The Tivoli theater was opposite when this c. early 1940s Dexter Silvercraft was published. The Silvercraft was a well-printed monochrome, not fitting the traditional categories, for which some collector interest has been shown in the recent past. (Collection of Cynthia Harris.)

AMERICAN TYPE FOUNDERS COMPANY, 300 COMMUNIPAW AVENUE, JERSEY CITY, N.J., U.S.A.

The 300 Communipaw Avenue plant of American Type Founders Company was reportedly the largest type foundry factory in the world, even when the sides of the building, later extended as shown in this c. 1920 card, were only six bays. They produced original designs, having an art department in the building, but the varieties in their stock was no doubt smaller than the typical computer word processing program of 1999. American Type Founders cut their own type on engraving machines they built. The staff is shown gathered for an unidentified event. The vacant plant stands, absent the step gable and window ornamentation. (Collection of Cynthia Harris.)

35

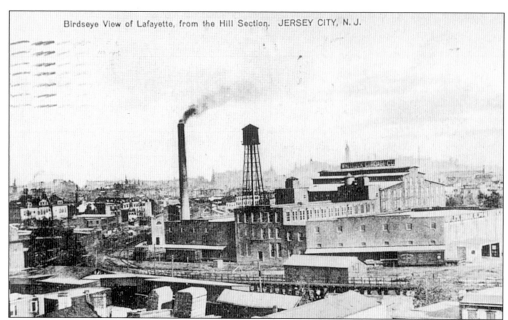

Looking east, one sees the tracks of the Lafayette branch of the Central Railroad in the foreground, a factor in the location of the plant of the Whitlock Cordage Company behind the rails. The firm, founded in Elizabethport in 1815, relocated to Brooklyn following an 1891 fire that destroyed its early New Jersey plant. (Collection of Cynthia Harris.)

Whitlock Cordage Co., Jersey City, N. J.

The Whitlock Cordage Company bought the former 10-acre site of the New Jersey Zinc Company at Communipaw Avenue and the Morris Canal. They built a new, electrically powered factory in 1905, complete with a generating system. The company's principal product was manila rope, which was made for marine use. It was formerly laid up on the ground, requiring a space 1,200-1,500 feet long, but modern equipment was then able to lay up rope in 5,000-6,000-foot lengths by machine. The Voigt No. 260 card is a c. 1909 view. The plant stands vacant. (Collection of Cynthia Harris.)

36

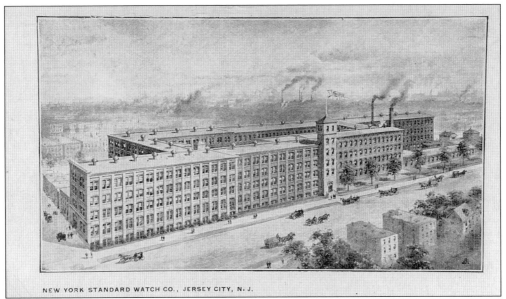

NEW YORK STANDARD WATCH CO., JERSEY CITY, N. J.

The New York Standard Watch Company factory, when photographed facing the narrow elevation on the south side of Communipaw Avenue at number 401, gave no suggestion of the extensive plant built in several sections that was located on Woodward Street and to the east. The card is a *c.* 1905 view. The corner site is now occupied by private houses, apparently built in the recent past. (Collection of Cynthia Harris.)

Corner Halladay and Lafayette Streets.   JERSEY CITY, N. J.

John Steck is probably the figure with the apron in front of his grocery at 311 Halladay Street, at Lafayette. His store published this card, which has the appearance of an early Albertype, *c.* 1908. The penned dates on the bottom are unexplained; one wonders if they reflect time in business, as many small grocers were succumbing to supermarket competition in the post-World War II years. (Collection of Cynthia Harris.)

37

All Saints Church was founded in 1896 as a part of St. Patrick's Parish, first celebrating Mass at Lafayette Battery Hall. A combination school and church was begun in the spring of 1897, completed in December, with the school opening in January 1898. The school was a success, reflecting the Reverend Joseph H. Meechan's belief that reaching the local Catholic community could be best accomplished through the children. The school's sisters occupied the building adjoining the school, presumably the c. 1870s Second Empire-style house at left in this c. 1908 Voigt card No. 29. Father Meechan's successful fund-raising paid for the school, permitted purchase of a rectory in 1901, and funded the construction of an elaborate church. (Collection of Cynthia Harris.)

All Saints Church was built at the southwest corner of Pacific and Communipaw Avenues c. 1910 and was designed by John T. Rowland Jr., associated with Frank Eurich Jr. The Gothic Revival church, built of North Carolina granite, measured about 90 by 170 feet. A 3,000-pound bell was installed in the main tower, which is 112 feet high. Three entrances with large, carved-oak doors were centrally located between the main and the octagonal tower on the east, which contained a baptistery; it rose to 70 feet. The seating space of 65 by 100 feet held nearly 1,000 worshippers. The exterior of the church, constructed by M.T. Connolly Contracting Company, is unchanged, but it is now occupied by the Cornerstone Church of Christ, following the merger of All Saints into the Assumption of the Blessed Virgin Mary Church at 344 Pacific Avenue. (Collection of Jersey City Public Library.)

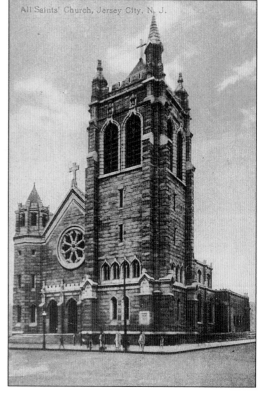

The west side of Pacific Avenue shows mixed styles of house architecture on this c. 1910 card (No. 217 of J.H. Grinnalds). The c. 1890s Colonial Revival at left may have been built on a lot separated from the c. 1860s Italianate place adjacent to it. All Saints (at right) dominates the landscape. (Collection of Cynthia Harris.)

The large, Italianate-style house at right (with a cupola in partial view) appears to be one of four built c. 1850s by Keeney & Halladay, early real estate developers who established the one-time residential character of Pacific Avenue. However, the Lafayette section was industrialized by the end of the 19th century. Identifying the view as "west" was aided by the sender who wrote "Van Horne" in the background of this c. 1908 Ernest Heiland card. (Collection of Cynthia Harris.)

The west side of Pacific Avenue, on the block south of Lafayette Street, is dominated by the Lafayette Methodist Church. Originated through weekly prayer meetings conducted in a school built in 1863 by shipbuilder M.S. Allison, the first church began in a structure on Allison's land. It was erected for political gatherings, permitted there with the proviso it revert to the Methodist Episcopal Society for a church after the 1868 campaign. (Collection of Cynthia Harris.)

Pacific Avenue, Jersey City, N. J.
Lafayette M. E. Church.

The same block at top is viewed looking north from Communipaw Avenue. Grandjean's Café at 304 Pacific Avenue demonstrates that decorative detail can enhance the prosaic store and apartment. The pictured church was begun in 1884 and dedicated May 3, 1885, under the pastorate of the church's first pastor, Reverend W.L. Hoagland, who returned for a second term after a 12-year absence. The card is a c. 1908 view. (Collection of Cynthia Harris.)

40

Note the prevalence of Belgian blocks in this early "paved" street. The author found a short street in the Lafayette neighborhood still paved in this manner. Driving over it in a modern sedan with a good suspension system was so jarring that he wonders how motorists could travel regularly over them.

Pacific Avenue Station of the Central R. R. of N. J. Jersey City, N. J.

The Pacific Avenue station (formerly Lafayette) was the second stop on the Newark and New York branch of the Central Railroad. Located just east of the Morris Canal, it is pictured on this c. 1909 Voigt 392. (Collection of Cynthia Harris.)

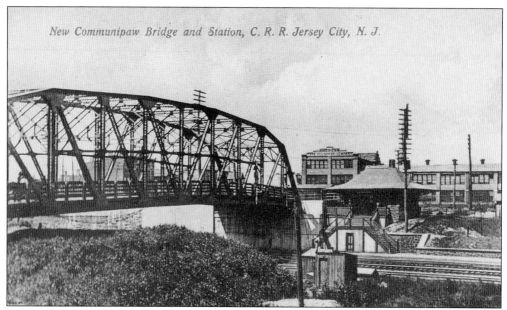

New Communipaw Bridge and Station, C. R. R. Jersey City, N. J.

The Communipaw station, the first outside the Central Railroad's terminal on the Hudson River, was located at the foot of Communipaw Avenue. Behind it is the American Type Founders building pictured on page 35. The bridge, "new" at the time of this c. 1908 card, can still be seen today west of the road at New Jersey Turnpike Extension, Exit 14B. It lost its land tie to the former Central Railroad rail facilities long ago. (Collection of Cynthia Harris.)

New Jersey's 1993 suit against New York to establish sovereignty over federally owned Ellis Island and overturn the terms of an 1834 compact between the two states was concluded by a 1998 decision, ruling that 90 percent of the island (or all of the part added to the original island by landfill) was New Jersey territory. New York retained 3.3 acres, including most of the three-story building in the foreground, which is the site of the immigration museum. Some of the border of the landfill can be seen as it follows the contour of the buildings at left.

Three

JOURNAL SQUARE AREA

FROM BERGEN SQUARE
TO FIVE CORNERS

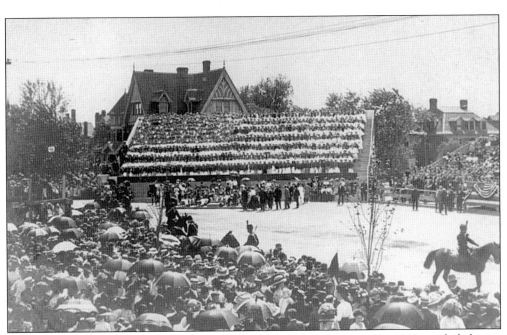

Jersey City Post Office employees Memorial Day parade on May 30, 1909, included over 1,700 girls attired in a manner to replicate a flag design when seated. (Collection Jersey City Public Library.)

The 250th anniversary of the settling of Bergen at Bergen Square was a major celebration in 1910. Many postcards were issued (the best of which were photographic views) of celebration events, extant historic structures (often with the addition of a souvenir slogan), and important buildings from the past. (Collection of Cynthia Harris.)

Bergen Ave. from Bergen Square, showing New Peter Stuyvesant Monument, Jersey City, N. J.

Bergen Square became intensively developed, especially after the construction of the broad plaza at the new Journal Square. This c. 1908 scene, looking north, still preserves some residential character, despite the presence of the then new and still-standing store and office at right. The background is a partial view of the *Jersey Journal* building, seemingly in the course of Bergen Avenue. (See page 48.) (Collection of Cynthia Harris.)

New and old Bergen Square mix in this c. 1912 card. The DeMott house formerly stood on the southeast corner of Bergen Avenue and Smith Street. A lot on the east side was set aside for education in the 17th-century layout of the square, but the historical record of schools from that period is obscure. The Odd Fellows Hall is the high-rise intrusion. (Collection of Cynthia Harris.)

JOHNSON CO., JERSEY CITY   Public School, No. 11.

"A SEAT FOR EVERY CHILD."

The Square's northeast corner with Academy Street has been home to the 1790 Columbia Academy and three public schools. The first was built in 1857, using some stones from the demolished Academy. The pictured building, erected in 1903, is seen on this c. 1905 commercial card, which Mayor Mark Fagan used as a campaign card to express his concern for a better school system. This building was destroyed by fire in 1966 and replaced with the present structure, which was named for Martin Luther King. The number was designated following Bergen's 1870 absorption into Jersey City. (Collection of Cynthia Harris.)

The 1666 Sip house, which stood at the southeast corner of Bergen Avenue and Newkirk Street, dates to the earliest days of the Bergen settlement. Its Dutch origin is recognizable by its sloping eaves. The house remained in the Sip family until 1924, but was lost to Jersey City due to commercial development and lack of local preservation interest. A proposal to move the house to West Side Park was rejected because of fears that the ancient structure could not survive the trip. However, an out-of-town buyer successfully moved the house to Westfield, Union County, where it stands today. (Collection of Jersey City Public Library.)

The main block of the Garrett Newkirk house appears to date from the last quarter of the 18th century, with the ell at right a 19th-century addition. It stood on Newkirk Street at Enos Place into the 1920s on a site that is now occupied by an office. (Collection of Jersey City Public Library.)

46

Lafayette reportedly visited here during the Revolution and dined under an apple tree. The tree later fell, and from it was fashioned a cane that was presented to Lafayette during his 1824 visit to America. The Van Wagenen home thus took the nickname "The Apple Tree House." The structure is the subject of ongoing research for proposed acquisition by Jersey City. It once served as a funeral home, but sits vacant in 1999. The image is an essay for a postcard by artist Richard La Rovere.

Northern Bergen Avenue became heavily commercialized following the opening of Journal Square into a plaza. The east side on the block from Sip Avenue to Newkirk Street reflects handsomely decorated, 1920s commercial architecture. The three-story building at right was built on the site of the Sip house. The card is a *c.* 1930 Manhattan Post Card Company monochrome. (Collection of Cynthia Harris.)

Journal Square was a largely residential area prior to 1920. Radical change and the absence of identifying detail make it difficult to locate this *c. 1920* white-border card with precision. (Collection of Cynthia Harris.)

The former *Jersey Journal* building was located on the northeast corner of the former course of Bergen Avenue and Sip Avenue. Its corner is opposite Bergen's route south of Sip, which the trolley in this *c. 1912* card is about to enter. The inset, taken from the 1919 *Hopkins Atlas of Hudson County*, suggests the locale. The removal of the *Jersey Journal* building permitted the transformation of Journal Square into an open plaza, a process that included the elimination of Wilkes Street. (Collection of Jersey City Public Library.)

This view of Sip Avenue, looking west from the still-standing Public Service building, helps reinforce perspective of the former Jersey Journal building, seen from another direction. The streets surrounding the Square became commercially desirable and were intensively developed, including the south side of Sip Avenue. (Courtesy of John Rhody.)

This 1940s linen card view of the Square (looking north) presents a scene that was remained unchanged for decades, until the 1970s construction of the Path Transportation Center, north of the extant commercial structures at right. (Collection of Cynthia Harris.)

This 1940s linen card view, looking south from the bridge over the railroad cut, shows the construction along Sip Avenue in the left background. Planners have grumbled about Jersey City's lack of a central downtown, a not unexpected result of the City's amalgamation from several towns. Journal Square, built only 50 years after the final consolidation, appears to have served adequately as a central focus, its faults notwithstanding. Recent development trends, however, have reconstructed the downtown waterfront area, nearly effacing in the process the rail and manufacturing origins of downtown's initial commercial importance, but attaining a new level of significance as an office center.

This 1930s image preserves the memory of miniature golf in Journal Square. One can imagine it was built to pay the land taxes while the owner awaited an opportunity for major construction, which may never have come, judging by the modest structure built later (see page 51). The Elks building at left lost some of its character with the remodeling of the ground floor for stores. The crude art work of this example illustrates the poor quality of postcard production during the white-border era. (Collection of Cynthia Harris.)

The China Clipper used a photographic card, made by the Grogan Photo Service in Chicago, to depict a thriving Journal Square and their modern restaurant, now seen as nostalgically art deco. Note on the facade the namesake airplane in neon, then in the Pacific service. The painting of bus lanes foretells Journal Square's future as a transportation hub. (Courtesy of John Rhody.)

"CHINA CLIPPER"
New Jersey's Most Modern American-Chinese Restaurant
46-49 Journal Square, Jersey City

The Journal Square station of the Hudson Tubes, to use the term of the PATH rail system that separates "old" and "new" Jersey Citites, was initially known as Summit Avenue. The same platform system that existed at the time of this *c.* 1912 card is still in use, although the platforms were lengthened in the 1970s construction project. The freight train at right conveniently points out the presence of the adjoining Pennsylvania Railroad tracks. (Collection of Jersey City Public Library.)

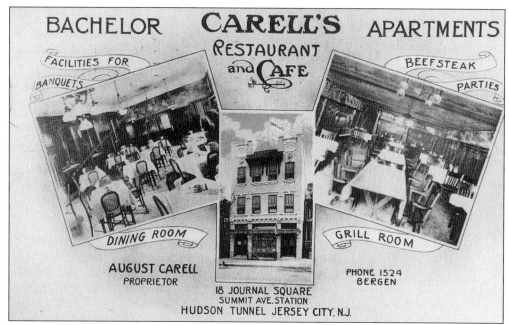

Carrell's was also a leading Journal Square hotel. It is uncertain as to whether this c. 1912 card promoting bachelor apartments and a restaurant reflected their main business or an ancillary facility. What is a beefsteak party, anyway? Perhaps something similar to the typical, outdoor cook-out of today? (Collection of Cynthia Harris.)

The 1924 construction of the Hotel Plaza at Sip Avenue and Enos Place reflected the rise of Journal Square as a commercial center. Designed by Clinton & Russell of New York, the 190-room hotel appealed to travelers to New York. On the back of the card, the hotel claims to be "The house of comfort—tourists headquarters—while visiting New York, make your home here and avoid the heavy traffic." The Plaza, which was later expanded, became a social center as well, but it closed in 1974. The place was remodeled as senior citizens' housing. (Collection of Jersey City Public Library.)

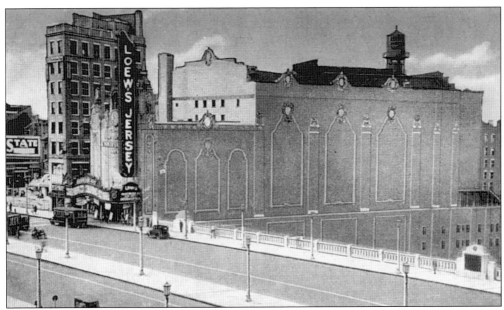

The Loew's Jersey, designed by Rapp and Rapp and built in 1929, is a premier example of the motion picture theater as entertainment palace. The 3,200-seat theater was built with an elaborate, Italian Baroque auditorium that was equipped with a Robert Morton pipe organ. The theater, saved after a lengthy preservation campaign, is being restored in 1999. It was built during the white-border postcard era and is typically seen on dismal cards, such as this *c.* 1930 view.

The Trust Company of New Jersey, founded in Hoboken in 1899, moved its main office to Jersey City with the *c.* 1920 construction of this 11-story, Italian Renaissance-style office designed by Clinton & Russell of New York. It was built at the southwest corner of Bergen and Sip Avenues. Following passage in 1913 of a law permitting consolidation of trust companies in New Jersey, the Bergen & Lafayette Trust Company (page 93), the People's Safe Deposit and Trust Company (page 67), and the Carteret Trust Company were merged into the Trust Company of New Jersey. The typical floor plan created pentagonal-shaped offices facing the Square and both side streets. The building still occupies the same corner and appears unchanged, although a major addition was built in the rear. Note the traffic officer in the kiosk at left. The image is a *c.* 1930 Manhattan Post Card Company monochrome. (Collection of Cynthia Harris.)

Kennedy Boulevard is the broad thoroughfare entering Journal Square in the middle of this late 1970s aerial view. Note the T-shaped Path Transportation Center at left. The rear extension of the Trust Company of New Jersey building is clearly visible at right. Note the PATH train at left and the Stanley Theater (with arched windows), above the bridge at left.

The Stanley Theater at 2932 Hudson (Kennedy) Boulevard, designed by Fred Wentworth, opened March 22, 1928. With over 4,300 seats, the Stanley was the largest theater in New Jersey. Motion picture exhibition ended in 1978, with audiences having dwindled to a mere handful. The card is a 1930 photograph. (Collection of Cynthia Harris.)

The Stanley was purchased by Jehovah's Witnesses in 1983, and the organization preserved and refurbished the building, while adapting it for spiritual use. They still offer tours of the place. The chrome card is a c. 1980s view showing a cleaned marquee that still glistens. (Collection of Jersey City Public Library.)

The elaborately decorated Stanley lobby contained vast allegorical murals painted by Hungarian-born artist Willy Pogany. Its main chandelier reportedly came from the old Waldorf-Astoria Hotel in New York, which was demolished for the construction of the Empire State Building. The auditorium, with a proscenium arch modeled after the Rialto Bridge in Venice, contained a Wurlitzer organ. The c. 1980s chrome post-dates the refurbishing. (Collection of Jersey City Public Library.)

Christian F. Mueller, who began his noodle and pasta business with a hand-manufacturing operation in Newark in 1867, moved to Jersey City in 1890 and built a factory on Boyd Avenue. This plant, designed by F.P. Sheldon & Son, was built c. 1914 at 180 Baldwin Avenue and was later expanded. Mueller's was purchased by the McKesson Corporation in 1976, which sold it to CPC International in 1983. They remained in Jersey City until the end of 1997, when they moved to Columbia, South Carolina. The back of this card announced Mueller's receiving a Grand Prize at the Panama-Pacific International Exposition in San Francisco, in 1915. (Courtesy of Steven Cohen.)

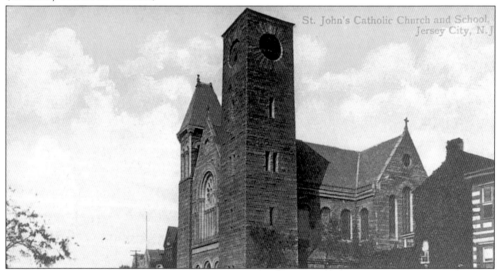

St. John the Baptist Roman Catholic Church was founded in 1884. It was, at first, a small frame church at Van Winkle and Huron Avenues. This Romanesque edifice, designed by George Palliser, was built in 1904 at Hudson (Kennedy) Boulevard and Van Winkle Avenue. The image on the card, published c. 1910 by Valentine, has been changed by the construction of a major addition to the south (square) tower, making it one of the tallest landmarks in the city. The church, listed on the National Register of Historic Places, is also known for its extensive collection of art mosaic. (Collection of Jersey City Public Library.)

This 1952 card publicized a live animal nativity scene "designed and constructed in the recreational centers of Jersey City . . . and made possible through the interest and cooperation of John V. Kenney, Mayor . . ." There was no question of a municipal Christmas display then, a subject that has been locally challenged in Jersey City since 1994. A 1999 Court of Appeals decision will permit continuation of the traditional displays as long as they are secularized by inclusion of Santa, Frosty the Snowman, a red sleigh, and a Kwaanza ribbon-decorated evergreen. No mention was made of Alvin and the other chipmunks.

The meeting of Summit, Newark, and Hoboken Avenues form a juncture known formally as Five Corners. The focus of this view, looking east, is the Jersey City Trust Company Neo Classical building. It used the configuration of the triangular corner, with Newark at right and Hoboken at left. The bank later merged into the Commercial Trust Company. St. Paul's Lutheran Church is at left. The Valentine card is a c. 1910 view. (Collection of Jersey City Public Library.)

Hudson County built this fine, Greek Revival courthouse on the south side of Newark Avenue, near Five Corners, in 1844. It was also near the site later chosen for the 1910 court, seen at left in the image below. The older structure was demolished after the new court was built. (Collection of Jersey City Public Library.)

This early-1960s chrome shows the 1910 court at left and the administration building at right. The former, designed by Hugh Roberts and richly decorated by many outstanding murals, was threatened with destruction until saved after a lengthy preservation campaign. The building, today the William J. Brennan Courthouse, was listed on the National Register of Historic Places in 1970. (Collection of Jersey City Public Library.)

Four

THE HEIGHTS

The Neo-Classical Jersey City High School, built in 1904 to a design by John T. Rowland Jr. at the northeast corner of Palisade and Newark Avenues, replaced the high school that conducted classes at the top floor of P.S. 5 on Bay Avenue. The building in this c. 1905 Lefferts photographic card is square in shape. A similar structure was added in a 1911 expansion, and the two met at a seven-bay center link, replacing one end of the old building, which was built under a larger and more elaborate triangular pediment. The school was named for William Leverett Dickinson, a Vermont native, who began his educational career in Jersey City as tutor to the J.D. Ward family, in 1838. He became superintendent of Jersey City schools in 1872 and was a force behind the founding of the high school that year. (Courtesy of John Rhody.)

The Jersey City Public Works Department was established in 1851 to address a water supply problem for the growing city. A reservoir on the heights was first filled with Passaic River water in 1854. A proposed expansion of the system was the subject of a massive political fraud in the 1870s. The Second Empire headquarters on the west side of Summit Avenue appears to be of c. 1870s origin. Behind it was Reservoir Number 2, now the site of a park and fire department headquarters. The stone walls at right contained Reservoir Number 3, part of which is Pershing Field. Other parts of this site are now undergoing development. The card is a c. 1907 view. (Collection of Cynthia Harris.)

A playground and athletic field were built on the site of former reservoir land. This c. 1906 card shows the interior of walls similar to the exteriors at top, and a number of still-standing buildings on the north side of Manhattan Avenue, including 84 and 82 (left and right respectively, over the subjects). Number 76 is recognizable despite its shingling, while the front-gabled number 74 was raised to two stories. (Collection of Jersey City Public Library.)

The east side of Central Avenue opposite the present Pershing Field is seen *c.* 1906. St. Nicholas Roman Catholic Church dominates the streetscape and shows the 1905 edifice of a parish founded in 1886. Hook & Ladder Company Number 3 is adjacent, on the south side of Ferry Street. The factory on the top of page 62 is seen here in its street context, left of the church. (Courtesy of John Rhody.)

The grounds of the former reservoir, facing Manhattan Avenue, were long used for recreational purposes. A costly project, they were built into a first-class park and athletic field, becoming the pride of the Jersey City system. The park was named for General John Joseph Pershing and was dedicated in 1922. Its rapidly attained stature was reflected in its choice for the 1924 Military Meet. The park, still in fine condition, is seen on this *c.* 1930 white border card; the rest house in the background has been replaced.

The Commercial Italianate factory of the Franco American Food Company, located on the southeast corner of Franklin Street and Central Avenue, was built c. 1895. It is shown here c. 1906, with St. Nicholas Church in the background. Franco American made soup there until 1922, when the operation was purchased by Campbell's. Vacuum tubes were manufactured in the plant in the late 1920s. The building was demolished in 1962 and a supermarket was built on the site. The card is Voigt No. 177. (Collection of Cynthia Harris.)

John Mehl & Company, founded in New York City in 1858, moved to Jersey City in 1882 and became one of the nation's leading manufacturers of leather goods, including pocket books. Their factory, viewed from the southeast corner of Webster Avenue and Hutton Street, was built in stages. The first 12 bays on Hutton (left) are apparently part of the original construction. Three additional bays are shown in this c. 1908 card (Voigt 91), while nine additional bays were added later. The once-vacant building, its exterior virtually unchanged, is undergoing renovation in 1999. (Collection of Cynthia Harris.)

Turnverin were German social clubs that focused on the promotion of health and physical culture; the first syllable came from the German "turnen," which means "to practice gymnastics." This hall at 156 Webster Avenue follows handsome classical lines. Its exact date is unknown, but the card is a c. 1906 view. The building no longer stands; its demise is suggested by the manufacturing building in its place, which bears a cornerstone from an unknown builder, "1854–1926." The front gabled building to the left of it is gone, but number 162 (adjacent) remains, although sided and stripped of its decoration. (Collection of Cynthia Harris.)

Hudson City Turn Hall, Webster Avenue, Jersey City. (R. Weigel, Jersey City.)

Charles Kaufmann's market at the northeast corner of Webster Avenue and Griffith Street remains a corner food store. The building, seen c. 1912, is recognizable, but has been sided and is missing its ornamentation. (Collection of Cynthia Harris.)

Central Avenue, the traditional shopping street running north-south through the former Hudson City, or the Heights, as the section is popularly known, still possesses many of its late-19th and early-20th-century buildings. This view, seen on a *c.* 1910 card, looks north from Bowers Street. The building at left was replaced by the one below, while the structure on the northeast corner at right was being refurbished, including the installation of new shingling, as this book was being completed in 1999. (Collection of Cynthia Harris.)

The *c.* 1912 Georgian Revival People's Safe Deposit and Trust Company branch of the Trust Company of New Jersey, located at the northwest corner of Central Avenue and Bowers Street, is one of Jersey City's most handsome commercial buildings. It is in fine condition and remains unchanged. The store adjacent was replaced by a substantial *c.* 1920s store and office that formerly housed a major variety store. (Special Collections & Archives, Rutgers University Libraries.)

The west side of Central Avenue, south of Bowers Street, remains a well-preserved block. Note the subtle change in the signs at the north corner; one sign reads "cheap cash grocer" in this *c.* 1905 card, but merely "cash grocer" on the top of page 64. The Central Avenue trolley was one of the earlier ones replaced by a bus line at some point around the 1920s. (Courtesy of John Rhody.)

Bowers Street is shown in this view looking from the corner at top. The largely intact street is dominated by the Central Avenue Reformed Church, located on the corner of Central Avenue when founded in 1871. The church structure on the left was completed in May 1894. Its cornerstone is dated 1893. (Collection of Cynthia Harris.)

The sun can be a bane or aid to street photography. Perhaps this *c.* 1906 scene of Central Avenue, looking north from Zabriskie Street, was photographed around noon so both sides would be illuminated by an overhead sun. Note Allers' clock. Most of the buildings remain, usually with cladding, painting, or storefront changes that range in quality from the acceptable to the dreadful. (Collection of Cynthia Harris.)

Mr. and Mrs. George Allers mailed their greetings in 1909 on a photographic card of their jewelry store at 306 Central Avenue. It is shown here decorated for an unspecified event. Photographing the east side is best done later in the afternoon, when the sun is behind the photographer. Notice not only the clock, but the eyes, which were repainted. They look less human and do not appear as large and penetrating as in the version at top. The sign is gone, of course; a clothing retailer now occupies the store. (Collection of Cynthia Harris.)

The People's Safe Deposit and Trust Company was founded in 1896 and opened at the southeast corner of Central Avenue and Hutton Street. This Neo-Classical building probably dates from that period. The now-dismal ground floor is extensively changed for retail occupancy, while both roof balustrades are gone. People's Safe Deposit merged into the Trust Company of New Jersey in 1913. The Central Avenue branch is pictured at the bottom of page 64. (Collection of Cynthia Harris.)

Arion Hall; Jersey City Heights

Arion Hall is located at 87 Hutton Street, at the southwest corner of Cambridge Avenue. The picture indicates a c. 1890 building (not as old as some claims), but an exterior clad in stucco and stripped of its ornamentation obscures evaluation. The building is now the Elks Hall; west of it is the Jersey City Masonic Center, another exterior marred by alterations. The c. 1906, undivided Voigt gives a suggestion of a business antecedent. (Collection of Cynthia Harris.)

Summit Avenue is a second commercial street with a lengthy north-south course through the Heights. The scene near North Street is stable today. The corner buildings to the left, at Irvine Street, suggest the importance of building ornamentation. The now-sided cornice on the south side detracts from the building's appearance, while well-preserved decorative detail on the north maintains the building's character. (Collection of Cynthia Harris.)

Booraem Ave., from Palisade Ave., Jersey City Heights. N.J.

A number of Second Empire-style houses on Booraem Avenue suggest the street was developed in the 1870s. The example at left (39 and 41) is well preserved and now possesses an enclosed porch. The Waverly Congregational Church (right) closed c. 1965. (Collection of Cynthia Harris.)

68

The implied message of E. Walter's meat market is surely, "Our diligent, efficient staff is ready to serve you." Although we have no way of measuring their usual business, the place seems particularly well stocked, and the Christmas decorations suggest a holiday peak period. (Collection of Cynthia Harris.)

The attractive, Romanesque Revival Public School Number 25 was built in 1892 at Columbia Avenue and Zabriskie Street. The school was expanded in 1912 with the construction of a second building to the east, facing the Boulevard. The pictured old section was demolished, and a new extension was built adjoining the 1912 building. The two structures comprise the school that remains today. (Special Collections and Archives, Rutgers University Libraries.)

An elevated trolley line ran through the Public Service Railway Company building at the northwest corner of Palisade Avenue and Ferry Street. It then proceeded east to begin a descent along a trestle running to the ferry at the Hudson Place Terminal, Hoboken. The building enclosing the track, which included a ticket office, is now the site of a supermarket and its parking lot, but the Public Service office building (right) still stands, occupied by Jersey City municipal offices. The card is a c. 1910 view. (Collection of Jersey City Public Library.)

The dramatic trestle was popular among card publishers; many scenes of it exist. Construction of the trestle, which reached a height of 125 feet, began in 1882. Service commenced in 1886, with cables pulling the first cars on a line that was electrified in 1892. Trolley service ended in 1949, their routes replaced by buses; the trestle was dismantled shortly thereafter. This image is an Illustrated Postal Card Company c. 1905 card. (Courtesy of John Rhody.)

Grand View Hall (its name when built) or the Jersey City Gardens (the hall's final name) is shown at left, at its location on the southwest corner of Franklin Street and Ogden Avenue. It is the most recognizable identification clue in this c. 1908 view of the Heights at top and Hoboken at bottom. Note Paterson Plank Road at right and how the street ascends the hill. Travel by foot was facilitated by the famed Franklin Street steps, located in the hill to the left of the L-shaped factory(center, near the inset). Both cards are from around 1908. (Inset: Collection of Cynthia Harris.)

The Lackawanna and Erie Railroads were separate lines when their tunnels crossed in the early years of the 20th century. The site is likely near the Boulevard crossing of the rails north of Journal Square. (Collection of Jersey City Public Library.)

This is a view looking north, with Hoboken at right under the hill. The tracks of the New Jersey Junction Railroad ran parallel to the Paterson Plank Road at this point. The trolley is the Summit Line. The *c.* 1907 scene is on Voigt 34. (Special Collections and Archives, Rutgers University Libraries.)

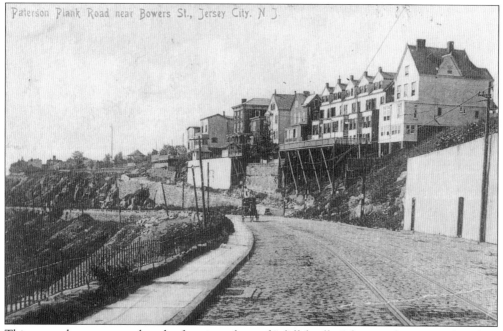

Paterson Plank Road near Bowers St., Jersey City, N. J.

This scene demonstrates that the facetious slang of "cliff dweller" for an urbanite can be taken literally at times. It may be difficult to spot the photographer's perspective today, as larger structures have replaced many present on this *c.* 1908 card. (Collection of Cynthia Harris.)

Five

BERGEN

The 10-foot-high, seated Lincoln was sculpted by James Earle Fraser and mounted on a 50-foot-wide, semi-circular base that was erected in 1929 at the entrance to West Side Park. The statue was unveiled and dedicated June 14, 1930. The project was sponsored by the Lincoln Association of Jersey City and paid in part by public subscription. The brooding figure named "Lincoln the Mystic," is one of the largest, and is widely recognized as one of the finest of the many Lincoln statues in America. The park was renamed Lincoln Park. The card is from the 1930s; the particular card illustrated was mailed in 1956 by Laura Underhill, wife of postcard publisher Irving, as an example of his work. (Collection of Cynthia Harris.)

The Fourth Regiment was organized in 1869, following authorization for a national guard to replace irregularly organized state militias. New Jersey's militia provided the origins of the Fourth Regiment, a group that served in various riot control activities. Their impressive Richardsonian Romanesque armory was completed in February 1895 at the southeast corner of Bergen Avenue and Mercer Street. Plans for a tall signal tower were never executed. Seen on this *c.* 1910 postcard, the armory was destroyed by fire on June 17, 1927. Hudson Catholic High School is now on the site.

The Carteret Club, a men's social organization founded in 1885, built this Romanesque-Shingle-style clubhouse on the northeast corner of Bergen Avenue and Mercer Street in the late 1880s. The place was purchased by St. Aedan's Church, which used it as a rectory. The Carteret built a new clubhouse at the southeast corner of the Boulevard and Duncan Avenue. This building, seen *c.* 1908 on Voigt 155, was demolished for construction of the present church. (Collection of Cynthia Harris.)

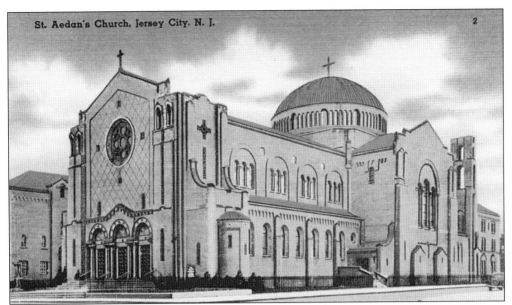

St. Aedan's Roman Catholic Church was founded in 1912. The congregation met in a temporary chapel, making an elementary school erected in 1913 on the west side of Tuers Avenue as their first building. The school's first floor was later used as a church, prior to the 1930–31 construction of this magnificent, Romanesque edifice on the northeast corner of Bergen Avenue and Mercer Street. Jersey City architect Edward A. Lehmann designed the church, while the exacting Father Roger A. McGinley supervised construction. A partial view of the rectory is at left on the only card known of St. Aedan's, a 1930s linen, which inadequately pictures one of Jersey City's finest architectural landmarks.

St. Dominic's Academy, founded in 1878 on First Street, had two other homes before the Dominican sisters acquired the Carteret Club's building, at the southeast corner of the Boulevard and Duncan Avenue, in 1941. Their elite, private girls' academy moved there in 1942. The school is seen on a 1940s Albertype pastel-tinted card. This style is the finest, widely issued card in the second quarter of the 20th century. (Collection of Cynthia Harris.)

The residential character of Bergen Avenue, north of Montgomery Street, is reflected on this *c.* 1910 card by Valentine. At left is a *c.* 1870s house, indicated on a later map as the John Winner estate, and two other houses south of the Bergen Reformed Church, on what would be a business block within 20 years. Phillips Hall, at the edge of Foye Place, is at right, in back of the Fourth Regiment Armory. (Collection of Cynthia Harris.)

Foye Place was one block connecting Montgomery Street to Bergen Avenue on an angle. It became the eastern edge of what was designated in the mid-1950s as McGinley Square, named for the founding priest of St. Aedan's, who "by erecting magnificent parochial buildings enhanced the beauty and dignity of the neighborhood," as quoted from the Square's bronze memorial plaque. The buildings in the background (which no longer stand today) appear to be the Foye Apartments. The waiting room, first used by trolley riders, was demolished in 1973. The card is a *c.* 1920s white border. (Collection of Cynthia Harris.)

The Bergen Reformed Church, the oldest church in New Jersey, was founded in 1660. It has occupied three church buildings, the first an octagonal structure at the southwest corner of Bergen Avenue and Vroom Street. It was replaced there in 1773 by a two-and-one-half-story gabled building with a tower and steeple. The present Greek Revival edifice, built in 1841 at the southwest corner of Bergen and Highland Avenues and one of Jersey City's best-known landmarks, was listed on the National Register of Historic Places in 1973. The building is unchanged from the c. 1908 Voigt Number 27 card, other than by a replaced balustrade. The Bergen Reformed parish has been in union since 1970, with the Trinity United Presbyterian Church, an amalgamation of three churches of that denomination. (Collection Jersey City Public Library.)

Both the Bergen Avenue landscape and the Masonic Temple have changed since they were first pictured on a Leighton & Valentine card, c. 1912. Highland Lodge completed the building at number 835 in 1911. Although the structure is recognizable, the columns have been covered or removed. A store and apartment now stand to the left. The south elevation of number 851 at Vroom Street is seen at right. The structure is now extended on the west, in the place of the two-and-one-half-story side-gabled house that appears to date from the first half of the 19th century. The former temple is the home of the Coptic orthodox patriarchate, St. George & St. Shenduda Church. (Collection of Jersey City Public Library.)

Bergen Avenue, looking north from Fairmount, was a busy intersection when pictured *c.* 1912 on Voigt 555, an infrequent example of that publisher in color. The building at right stands, without its luster of the past, while most of the frame structures on the west side have been replaced, with the large signs of their stores often concealing their origins and detail. (Collection of Cynthia Harris.)

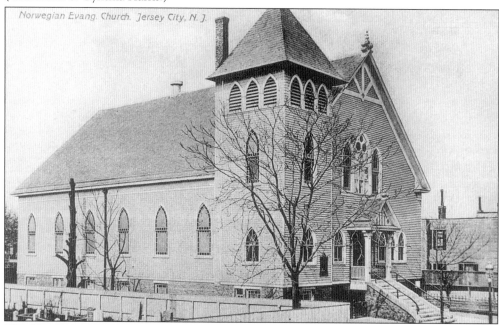

Norwegian Evang. Church. Jersey City, N. J.

The Norwegians, among Jersey City's numerous ethnic groups, had the Norsk Evangelical Lutheran Church as their house of worship. This Gothic Revival edifice was built in the late 19th century at 155 Vroom Street, the location giving rise to the congregation's present name of the Vroom Street Evangelical Free Church. The *c.* 1908 card is Voigt 140. (Collection of Cynthia Harris.)

78

The Beaux Arts Young Men's Christian Association building, designed by John F. Jackson, was erected in 1924 at 654 Bergen Avenue. The place, remaining a YMCA into the 1990s, is now a residence run by New Hope Housing. The exterior is unchanged, but plans have been made to do extensive interior remodeling that will convert individual rooms into efficiency apartments. The buildings at left remain; their facades have been altered with siding and grade-level stores. (Collection of Cynthia Harris.)

The Right-Heights Realty Company office at 721 Bergen Avenue is seen covered with bunting, probably for the 250th anniversary of Bergen celebration, on this photographic card. (Collection of Cynthia Harris.)

John Tise built this tavern *c.* 1815 at the southwest corner of Bergen and Glenwood Avenues, on the site of the former Eagle Tavern. The latter, dating from the 1750s, was well-frequented in the stage era of travel by coaches heading west along Communipaw Avenue to Newark. A Washington visit is a rumor, but any possible brief stay would hardly have constituted headquarters status.

The Second Empire Robert Percy house was built *c.* late 1870s at 70 Glenwood Avenue and the northeast corner of Hudson (Kennedy) Boulevard. It was called the Moose clubhouse at the time of this *c.* 1910 card. The building was demolished *c.* 1915 to make way for an apartment house. (Collection of Cynthia Harris.)

The former Edward F.C. Young house, at the southwest corner of the Boulevard and Glenwood Avenue, is one of the city's most often illustrated buildings. It was home to one of Jersey City's major financiers and industrialists. The nearly pastoral street, now heavily developed, is seen on this *c.* 1906 Lefferts photographic card. (Collection of Cynthia Harris.)

This *c.* 1910 Highland Avenue view, may be on the Boulevard, but development makes identification difficult. (Collection of Cynthia Harris.)

The Jewish Community Center, founded *c.* 1918 at Summit and Sip Avenues, built this Italian Renaissance Revival-style headquarters in 1928 at the northeast corner of Bergen and Belmont Avenues. It was home to a myriad of social, athletic, and cultural activities. Dances were popular entertainment, while basketball was the center's most intensely competitive sport. Rabbi Plotkin's Hebrew school was an educational draw. Membership declined in the 1950s due to the suburbanization of the city's once-thriving Jewish population; the center closed in 1980, the building later demolished. The site is now home to Joseph H. Brensinger Public School Number 17, dedicated September 30, 1995. (Collection of Cynthia Harris.)

The Emory Methodist Church, founded in 1863, built its first church on Ivy Place that year. This Gothic building, seen *c.* 1910, was erected on the northwest corner of Bergen and Belmont Avenues in 1905; it still stands, virtually unchanged. The congregation thrived for decades but sold the building *c.* 1967 to the A.M.E. Zion Methodist Church, which was founded in 1840. (Collection of Jersey City Public Library.)

Public School Number 17 was built in 1898 on the north side of Duncan Avenue, near West Side Avenue. Presumably made up of eight rooms and offices, it appears to be a bridge between the three-story, Italianate-style buildings that made up most early post-consolidation (1870) city schools and the larger, Beaux Arts-style buildings designed by John T. Rowland Jr. Rowland designed many of these buildings during his lengthy tenure as the board of education's supervising architect. The building in this view became a preschool, following the 1995 opening of the new P.S. 17 on Bergen Avenue. (Collection of Cynthia Harris.)

The east side of the Boulevard is shown c. 1905, with architect John T. Rowland Jr.'s Tudor Revival-style house at left. Adjoining it is the home of John Headden Jr. The two houses were probably the work of the same architect. The latter house still stands, but the Rowland place on the southeast corner of Belmont Avenue was replaced by an apartment house. (Collection of Cynthia Harris.)

Gifford Avenue became one of Jersey City's finest residential streets. A glimpse of the John Headden Jr. house on the northeast corner of the Boulevard is at left. Two houses separate it from the fine Colonial Revival of Henry W. Bishop. (Collection of Cynthia Harris.)

Extensive apartment construction makes tracing early Jewett Avenue images problematical. A fine row of Colonial Revival houses can be seen in this c. 1908 view. The one at right with the intersecting gambrel gables is especially interesting. (Collection of Cynthia Harris.)

Apartment construction on the Boulevard accelerated in the 1920s, changing its character from large private houses to substantial structures of several stories. A noteworthy one is the Sevilla Apartments, a Spanish Mission Revival influenced place at number 2801, the northwest corner of Sip Avenue, the former site of the home of Dr. Horace Bowen. The cornerstone is dated 1925; the apartments were ready for rental in early 1928. The card dates shortly after completion.

Bentley Avenue, one of the finer residential streets in the city, runs two blocks from Bergen to West Side Avenue. Thus, the cross intersection makes one believe this c. 1910 scene is at the Boulevard. (Collection of Cynthia Harris.)

Hudson County Park. Jersey City, N. J. Entrance from Boulevard.

Belmont Avenue was closed from the Boulevard to West Side Avenue, and many of its structures were moved to permit this east entrance to West Side Park, labeled "Hudson County" for its builder, on this *c.* 1909 Voigt card number 610. The new St. Aloysius Church is in the background, while the future site of the Lincoln statue is behind the man. Also see pages 73 and 99.

Parmly Memorial Baptist Church, Fairmount Ave. Jersey City, N. J.

The First Baptist Church was organized as the Union Free Baptist Church of Jersey City in 1848. The name was changed to the former in 1868 and the church occupied a building on Grove Street. It was renamed again for longtime pastor, the Reverend Wheelock H. Parmly, D.D., following his death in 1894, as the Parmly Memorial Church. The church relocated to the southeast corner of Hudson (Kennedy) Boulevard and Fairmount Avenue, building this Gothic-influenced edifice designed by A.F. Licht, begun in 1909 and dedicated on June 19, 1910. The well-preserved, little-changed church still stands. The congregation merged with the Bergen Baptist Church in 1945 and became First Baptist once again. (Collection of Jersey City Public Library.)

St. Patrick's Roman Catholic Church, founded in 1869, was led in its early years by the Reverend Patrick Hennessey, born March 17, 1833, in Limerick, Ireland, who had earlier been pastor of St. Patrick's in Elizabethport. They acquired that year a plot on Bramhall Avenue, running from Ocean to Grand Avenues, and anticipated growth by planning this huge, Gothic edifice designed by Patrick C. Keely of Brooklyn. The cornerstone was laid November 13, 1870, and the church dedicated August 19, 1877. St. Patrick's, the largest church in Jersey City, has a number of educational and spiritual buildings around the main church; the well-preserved complex was listed on the National Register of Historic Places in 1980. (Collection of Jersey City Public Library.)

The bell-domed tower on the Romanesque-style Arlington Avenue depot made it one of the more attractive stations on the Central Railroad Newark and New York branch. It is seen c. 1910 on Voigt 362. (Collection of Cynthia Harris.)

The Jersey City Hospital originated by 1868 at Paulus Hook. The City purchased a former country estate at Montgomery Street and Baldwin Avenue in 1881, completing a new hospital in December 1882. The illustrated brick building, three stories with five-story towers when built, was completed in 1909 and expanded later, including the construction of a second building in 1919, slightly larger, connected by a wing. The former P.S. 36, which was erected in 1918 and became the A. Harry Moore School for Crippled Children in 1925, was turned into the Hospital for Contagious Diseases in 1931. The Margaret Hague Maternity Hospital, later the largest in the world, was begun in 1928 and completed in 1931. The surgical building, completed in 1931, is the high rise.

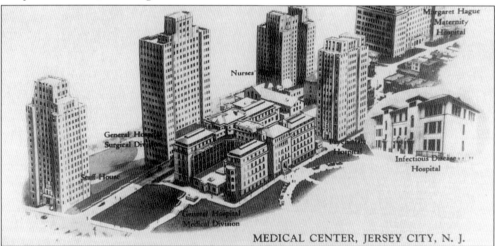

MEDICAL CENTER, JERSEY CITY, N. J.

The facility was designated the Jersey City Medical Center in 1930. The 1909–1919 hospital (top) is shown in relationship to the high-rise construction that was virtually continual in the 1930s. The school mentioned at top was demolished in 1934. The staff residence and nurses' buildings were completed in 1932. The card was issued by the City c. 1932 to help promote civic pride. Extensive construction followed, and the third phase of expansion was not completed until 1941. Changing medical services have transformed the Center considerably. The fine collection of Art Deco buildings, designed by John T. Rowland Jr., was placed on the National Register of Historic Places in 1985. (Collection Special Collections and Archives, Rutgers University Libraries.)

Borden's Condensed Milk Co., Jersey City, N. J.

Borden's was probably the best-known brand of the several milk processors active in Jersey City around 1900. They had two plants, including the one at 641 Montgomery Street, seen *c.* 1908 on Voigt 13. This plant was modernized or replaced, and Borden's facility there lasted until the 1960s. (Collection of Jersey City Public Library.)

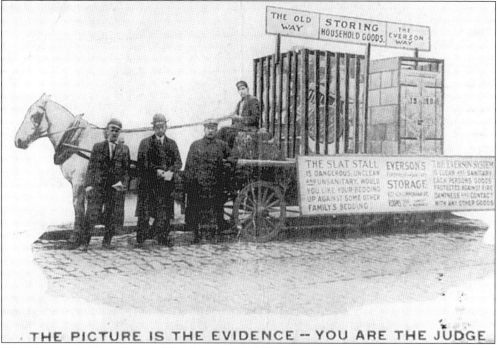

W.S. Everson & Sons Storage Warehouse at 622 Communipaw Avenue used a scare tactic to impress prospects on an early, perhaps *c.* 1915, advertising card. Apartment builders later addressed the problem of excess or seasonal household contents with basement storage bins, used perhaps into the early 1960s during an era of trust. (Collection of Cynthia Harris.)

This Scottish Rite Masonic Temple was built *c.* 1908 at 17 Park Street, near Harrison Avenue, designed in the Beaux Arts style by John T. Rowland Jr. Its substance and cost reflect the strength of free masonry at the time, a period when Jersey City supported several Masonic organizations. This group sold the building *c.* 1970 and moved to Livingston, New Jersey. It was occupied as offices by the Jersey City Board of Education in recent years. (Courtesy of John Rhody.)

The Jersey City Athletic Club was founded in 1878, joining the National Association of Amateur Athletics the next year and building this clubhouse in 1886 at the northwest corner of Clinton and Crescent Avenues. The unknown architect drew motifs from various styles current at the time, including Shingle, Queen Anne, and Tudor Revival. The club fell on hard times in the WW I era and became bankrupt. The building was sold to the Masonic Club of Jersey City, which was forced to sell the property, seen here *c.* 1910, in 1974.

Hasbrouck Institute, Jersey City, N. J. Adolie Seabrolee

Peter Hasbrouck founded the private Hasbrouck Institute in 1866 after teaching for a Van Vorst Township school, initially leasing the Lyceum on Grand Street. A growing school occasioned his successors to build this Romanesque Revival school on the former Bonnell estate at Crescent, Harrison, and Communipaw Avenues in 1892. The City purchased the building, using it for Lincoln High School while their building was erected on adjacent ground in 1919, demolishing the older building after Lincoln opened. The card was published by Illustrated c. 1905.

Lincoln High School, the second of the City's high schools, was designed by John T. Rowland Jr. and opened in 1919 on the corner of Crescent and Harrison Avenues. The evening, commercial high-school program was moved here in 1928. The Manhattan Post Card Company card is a c. 1930 view.

The Monticello Theater was built c. 1910 on the southeast corner of Monticello and Harrison Avenues, serving as a neighborhood movie house until c. 1960. The building is still there and the upper story is readily recognizable. The place is now the Miracle Temple, a Pentecostal church. (Collection of Jersey City Public Library.)

Charles A. was the third Cole to open a Jersey City drugstore. Is that him at the door? His store is at the northeast corner of Monticello and Harrison Avenues. The triangular pediments, brackets, and round-arch, attic windows give an unusual artistic finish to the typically prosaic frame store and dwelling. It survived at least into the 1960s, with the corner now cleared. The gelatin photo card published c. 1915 by Fred Thoele has the appearance of an early Albertype. (Collection of Cynthia Harris.)

The early-20th-century significance of Monticello Avenue as a business and shopping street is inferred from its choice as location for a new financial institution, the Bergen and Lafayette Trust Company, founded in 1902. This handsome, Neo-Classical building was opened that year, on the southeast corner with Brinkerhoff Street. The organization grew, but was merged into the Trust Company of New Jersey in 1913, the year a New Jersey law permitted consolidation of trust companies. The unchanged building remains there and is now a branch office. The site of the adjacent structure on this c. 1906 Charles Lefferts photographic card is a parking lot. (Collection of Cynthia Harris.)

Monticello Avenue is seen here, looking north from Brinkerhoff Street, where Walter Archbold and Charles F. Gallagher had a grocery store in a still-standing, but much-altered building. The fish sign refers to Emmanuel Britten's shop next door. The trolley was the Pacific Avenue Line, which ran from Exchange Place to Journal Square.

93

The first Public School Number 14 was built at 153 Union Street, between Sackett Street and Jackson Avenue (Martin Luther King Drive) in 1869. The mansard tower gives the handsome, Italianate-style building a touch of the Second Empire. The 1871 *Manual of the Board of Education of Jersey City* indicated the school was divided into three departments, each headed by a principal, with a total of eight "assistants" or teachers. The "janitrix" was paid more than seven of the eight teachers. A late-20th-century, former P.S. 14 teacher lent this Lefferts photographic card. (Collection of Cynthia Harris.)

The second Public School 14 in the Beaux Arts style was built east of the earlier one in 1908. The two co-existed for decades but were not connected. They were demolished in 1952 and replaced by the third school, which opened in 1954. (Collection of Cynthia Harris.)

Jackson Avenue was a major commercial and shopping street spanning the Bergen and Greenville sections. This *c.* 1909 view is looking north from the railroad cut, the traditional border (see page 106). A number of the buildings are standing, although the east side block to the south has been leveled for a station on the Hudson-Bergen Light Rail Transit System (its name at the time of this book). The street was renamed Martin Luther King Drive *c.* 1968. (Collection of Cynthia Harris.)

The Romanesque style edifice at the northwest corner of Madison and Clinton Avenues, appearing to have been built *c.* 1870, was initially the Bergen Baptist Church, a congregation that merged into the First Baptist in 1945 (see page 86). The well-preserved church, seen on a *c.* 1906 Lefferts photographic card, is now the Salem Baptist Church. The tall steeple is in place, although the dome of the north tower is missing. A parking lot exists in place of the adjoining house, while a tall, commercial structure was built on Madison on the spot pictured at the right edge. (Courtesy of John Rhody.)

The South Bergen Reformed Church, founded in 1874, was the antecedent of the First Congregational Church, which built this massive Richardsonian Romanesque church at the southwest corner of Bergen and Boyd Avenues in 1892–94. It could seat about 1,000 people and was dedicated February 11, 1894. The organization once had the reputation as the "elite" congregation of Jersey City, an impression reinforced by the imposing edifice, but a diminishing group sold it in 1970. The church is now the Cotton Temple Church of God in Christ. The houses at right on this *c.* 1907 Voigt 18 were replaced by a small, brick apartment. (Collection of Cynthia Harris.)

The People's Palace was a clubhouse and recreation center funded by Joseph Milbank. It was built by the Congregational Church in 1903, at the northeast corner of Bergen Avenue and Forrest Street. It contained a gym, track, rooms for various sporting activities, bowling alleys, billiard tables, and rifle and pistol ranges. Also present were two lodge rooms, a ball room, a theater, and a banquet hall. The elaborate facility was dedicated to humanity and intended to provide a wide variety of recreation for a modest cost. The card is a *c.* 1905 view. (Courtesy of John Rhody.)

This southerly view of Bergen Avenue from Boyd Street places the two structures on page 96 in their street context. The early success of the People's Palace is reflected by a three-bay addition on the south. The place was bought by the Catholic Youth Organization in 1941, which operated a recreation hall for years; they sold it to the City in 1973 for $500,000. The building had been vacant for some years prior to its demolition around the early 1990s. The site is an empty lot in 1999. The card is a *c.* 1906 Lefferts photograph. (Collection of Cynthia Harris.)

The non-denominational Church of the First Born was located at the southwest corner of Ocean and Bramhall Avenues. Worship practice is hinted by this example, in a note sent to Sister Mitchell in 1909. The sender writes, "we are taught to live God's word and to fight the good fight of faith and lay hold of eternal life." (Courtesy of John Rhody.)

The original Public School Number 24, appearing to have been built c. 1880, was located on the north side of Virginia Avenue, near West Side Avenue. It was destroyed by fire January 22, 1913. John T. Rowland Jr. designed a much larger Beaux Arts replacement (where the author learned to write), built in 1914 and dedicated May 4, 1915. The lessons of the fire brought new, tougher school standards. Auditoriums were on the grade floor, staircases were enclosed, and construction was of the fire-resistive type. The Lefferts photographic card dates c. 1907. (Collection of Cynthia Harris.)

Ege Avenue, looking west, is viewed from a perspective a few yards off the Boulevard. The roofs of the two houses at left, the gambrel at number 175, and the conical tower adjacent at 177, reflect the overlap of the Colonial Revival and Queen Anne styles during the late 1890s. The house at the far right was probably removed for the 1922 construction of Our Lady of Victories Roman Catholic Church. Next to it is number 176, with a barely perceptible gambrel roof. (Collection of Jersey City Public Library.)

Six

WEST SIDE

West Side Park at Night

The Hudson County Park Commission was appointed by the Court of Common Pleas to establish a county park system, obtaining $4.5 million in funding for acquisition and construction. The jewel of the system was the approximately 208-acre West Side Park, much of it built on the former Glendale Woods, to a design by landscape architects Charles Lourie and Daniel W. Langston. The park's name was taken from its locale, extending westward from West Side Avenue to the Hackensack River border. The occasion for its lighting was not identified on this c. 1910 photographic card. The time exposure made the brightest lights a large blur. Also see pages 73 and 86. (Collection of Jersey City Public Library.)

The West Side Avenue (formerly West Bergen) station of the Newark and New York branch of the Central Railroad, the final stop prior to crossing Newark Bay, was located on the east side of West Side Avenue, north of the tracks. The building, perhaps c. 1890s, is not without decorative charm, including jerkinhead gables on the sides and vergeboard on the front gable. It was demolished c. late 1940s, after the termination of passenger service. The area near the former station is undergoing extensive construction for a western branch station on the new light rail line. The Lefferts photographic card is a c. 1905 view. (Collection of Jersey City Public Library.)

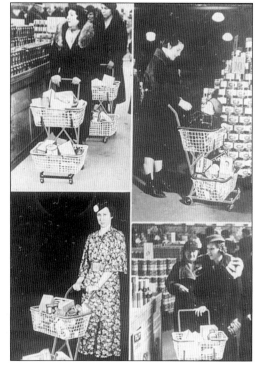

American Wire Form Company, located at Grant and West Side Avenues, promoted in the late 1930s their "NoGerm" baskets and carriers as a state-of-the-art business builder, claiming "Customers buy 2 baskets full instead of 1." This probably did not include customers with children (such as the one in the upper right corner, who seems to be filling an entire basket). Their pre-printed advertisement filled one-half of the message space on back. Jersey City has stayed in the vanguard of shopping cart developments, with a 1997 ordinance authorizing authorities to impound abandoned carts and levy a $50 fine on those using them outside of stores' parking lots. (Courtesy of John Rhody.)

The West Side Avenue Methodist Church, organized in a private home in 1871, quickly raised construction funds to lay its cornerstone that year. The basement at the northwest corner of West Side and Clark Avenues was completed in 1872 and the sanctuary was completed in 1888. The church, now faced in white brick, contains a new enclosure on its entrance on the facade. The steeple on the south tower is gone, as are the finials on the north. St. Mark's Day Care Center occupies the house on the right. The photographic card dates c. 1906. (Collection of Cynthia Harris.)

The 1936 erection of a first-rate athletic field was a principal Jersey City W.P.A. project; it was named Roosevelt Stadium for its benefactor. Located on Newark Bay at Droyers Point, the park was home to International League baseball, high school sports, and a variety of events. The stadium received its widest attention in 1956 and 1957, when the Brooklyn Dodgers played about seven home games there each season. Local authorities, thinking the Brooklyn flirtation was a possible presage of a move to the city, celebrated their new tenants' arrival, even closing schools the afternoon of the first contest. The stadium, which was also home to a fire-training school, became shabby in its later years and was demolished in 1985 for the construction of housing. (Collection of Cynthia Harris.)

Our Lady of Mount Carmel Roman Catholic Church, founded in 1905 in a vacant church structure, built this white brick edifice of Romanesque influence at the southeast corner of Broadway and Giles Avenue in 1926, to reflect changing demographics in the city's Italian population. The famed Father Artioli began a 33-year pastorate in 1936, having arrived in 1934 soon after Father Moscati was killed by an assassin. This card, printed by the Albertype Company of Brooklyn, shows the Holy Name Service Celebration of October 10, 1943. Note the temporary service memorial, which was replaced by a permanent monument erected Memorial Day, May 30, 1947. The rectory is pictured at left. (Collection of Cynthia Harris.)

St. Aloysius' Church was founded in 1897, first celebrating Mass at Donohue's Hall on May 30, 1897. The structure at right on this c. 1910 card was built in 1897–98 as a combination church and school, while the church at left was built in 1907–08. The building on West Side Avenue, designed by Charles Edward, draws on many stylistic influences and remains well-preserved and unchanged. (Collection of Jersey City Public Library.)

Robert V. Smith published in 1909 a postcard of his pharmacy at the southeast corner of West Side and Duncan Avenues. The building is quite recognizable; although little has changed in the upper stories, the grade level has been altered by bricking in the windows, part of the remodeling shown by its present medical office occupant. (Collection of Cynthia Harris.)

The Brunswick Laundry's massive plant served not only a commercial clientele, but appealed to the housewife with claims of their ability to lighten the burdens of domestic care. Some may remember their quaint, electric-powered route trucks, which survived into the 1950s. The card dates c. 1926, following the completion of a major expansion, which gave the owners the claim of the largest laundry in the world. Brunswick was sold to the Little Falls Laundry in 1963, which closed the plant of the 64-year-old Brunswick firm. The place was remodeled for residential use. The Brunswick Tower condominiums opened in 1986. (Collection of Cynthia Harris.)

Good promotion proclaims superlative qualities. However, the reader may wonder if Starr's Long Bar, at 854 Newark Avenue, claiming its full 82-foot length was the longest bar in the city, was distinctive or dubious. The card is one of a number of *c.* 1940s monochromes the place published. (Collection of Cynthia Harris.)

The Pulaski Skyway is too narrow, too filled with pot holes, and too often congested. It is also one of the engineering marvels of its day. Begun in 1930 and completed in 1932, the 3.6-mile, elevated highway designed and engineered by Sigvald Johanneson provided the first speedy connection between Newark and Jersey City by spanning the Passaic and Hackensack Rivers by two 1,250-foot, steel-cantilever bridges 145 feet above the water, and by overcoming difficult marshy terrain for its construction. Most of the structure consists of numerous, short-span Pratt deck trusses. The road, part of U.S. Highway 1, is named for General Casimir Pulaski, a Polish nobleman who fought for the colonists in the Revolution. He died from his wounds in 1779, following the Battle of Charleston. The Mayrose card dates *c.* 1940.

104

Seven

GREENVILLE

A truck and driver for the Du Bois Brothers Milk Company, 581 Ocean Avenue, is seen at an unidentified location, c. 1910. As quaint as this scene seems today, a motorized milk truck of a type with a few examples still on the road, will likely seem just as quaint 50 years from now. The author has a milk box used for home delivery prior to buying his place 28 years ago. The milk box has not seen a dairy product in that period, but sure is a useful delivery box for personally delivered "mail" and other objects. (Collection Jersey City Public Library.)

The Newark and New York Railroad, which opened in the 1860s, ran across southern Jersey City, spanning Newark Bay with a long bridge to Kearny. Some of its route was a sub-grade cut, as seen on this c. 1905 view looking east, towards Bergen and Jackson (Martin Luther King Drive) Avenues (the latter is the station in the rear). Passenger service was abandoned, following a period of shuttle service, after a 1946 ship collision made the bridge inoperative. New tracks are in place for the light rail system under construction in 1999.

The west side of Jackson Avenue, looking south from Virginia Avenue, shows the Jackson Avenue station built over the cut containing the tracks, as illustrated at top. The light rail tracks have been raised 17 feet to grade and now cross the street at this point; the extent of the rail-raising project is suggested by the inset. Some buildings on the west side remain (the one next to the bank is gone), but the entire east side block has been leveled for a new station. The card dates c. 1915, and the inset c. 1908. (Collection of Cynthia Harris.)

The Claremont Bank, founded on Ocean Avenue, was located on Jackson Avenue, adjacent to the railroad station (*c. 1912*) in this small but handsome Neo Classical-style building that banks favored for the first third of the 20th century. The structure was expanded and the bank merged into the Trust Company of New Jersey. The building is recognizable, with four Ionic pilasters across its facade. It is now occupied by St. Matthew's Baptist Church. (Collection of Jersey City Public Library.)

Halperin & Co. Pharmacy 427 Jackson Avenue, Jersey City N. J.

The old, colored-water-filled globes would have identified Samuel Halperim's shop as a pharmacy even without the sign. A business listing labeled them as "Careful Druggists." One hopes they did not have to distinguish themselves from careless competitors. Changes make it hard to ascertain if a store standing near the Forrest Avenue intersection is the one pictured. (Special Collections and Archives, Rutgers University Libraries.)

Henry Snyder Junior High School opened at Bergen and Myrtle Avenues September 1, 1914, the first of a projected group of junior high schools. Named for a former superintendent of schools who also co-authored a history of New Jersey, the Beaux Arts building designed by John T. Rowland Jr. (which spans the block to the Boulevard), was converted to high school use *c.* 1934 and still serves as one. The view on this *c.* 1930 Manhattan Post Card Company monochrome is the southeast corner. The lot on the left has been filled with Public School Number 41, built in 1966. (Collection of Cynthia Harris.)

The cornerstone of Public School Number 20 is dated 1899, but the Italian Renaissance Revival-influenced building at 160 Danforth Avenue, designed by C. Frederick Long, was dedicated on January 25, 1901. The little-changed building, running a full block to Cator Avenue, contains a bronze tablet memorial to Jacob C. Reinhart (November 18, 1831–July 27, 1904), who served as principal for 37 years. A leaded glass (many panes are stained) dome is a rare and outstanding architectural feature. Saving the venerable building is one of Jersey City's most urgent preservation concerns. (Collection of Cynthia Harris.)

The A. Harry Moore School for Crippled Children, designed by John T. Rowland Jr., was built in 1931 on the east side of Hudson (Kennedy) Boulevard at Culver Avenue, replacing a school founded in 1921 in the former P.S. 36, on the grounds of the Medical Center. It is named for the former Parks Commissioner who was elected governor for three-year terms in alternate elections of 1925, 1931, and 1937 (effectively as a stand-in for Frank Hague), who had a special interest in educating the handicapped. The school, acclaimed for the thoroughness of its facilities, is seen is this 1930s linen card. It stands unchanged, although the sign was moved to the facade.

New Jersey State Normal School, built at 2039 Hudson (Kennedy) Boulevard at the southwest corner of Culver Avenue, opened in 1929. The Collegiate Gothic-style building, now known as Hepburn Hall, was designed by Guilbert & Betelle, one of New Jersey's foremost school architects during the first third of the 20th century. The building stands little changed as the center of a school long-known as Jersey State College (or Jersey State Teachers College), which was re-designated New Jersey City University in 1998. Other buildings now surround it, as seen on its east facade in this c. 1950s glossy version of a card first issued as a linen. The view possesses neither the charm of a linen nor the clarity of a chrome.

Although the Reverend John C. MacErlain's alcoholic sanitarium and the MacErlain Institute from 1899 and 1902 respectively, may be considered antecedents of Sacred Heart, the church as a parish was approved by Bishop John J. O'Connor in 1905. This Gothic Revival church, built on the north side of Bidwell Avenue, about 500 feet from the corner of Jackson, was opened in 1908. Sacred Heart School followed in 1913. (Collection of Cynthia Harris.)

The Dominican Friars were given Sacred Heart Parish in 1920 and began planning a new church. This magnificent, Spanish Gothic-style edifice was built on the northeast corner of Bidwell and Jackson Avenues (Martin Luther King Drive), the site of the Institute, where it stands today as one of New Jersey's architectural treasures. The building was designed by Ralph Adams Cram, one of America's foremost ecclesiastic architects, who followed Dominican building principles and chose Spanish style motifs since St. Dominic was a Spaniard. The stained-glass, rose window was designed by Wright Goodhue. The Sacred Heart rectory became a priory in 1939. (Collection of Cynthia Harris.)

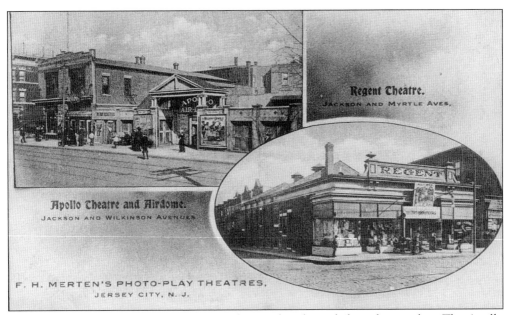

The airdome was an early open-air movie theater that depended on the weather. The Apollo was replaced by the enclosed New Apollo, which served as a neighborhood movie house into the 1950s. The building still stands. No trace was found of the Regent, but one owner with two theaters two blocks apart could be called a precursor of today's multi-screen operations. (Collection of Cynthia Harris.)

This attractive Beaux Arts store and apartment erected c. 1905 on the northwest corner of Jackson (Martin Luther King Drive) and Myrtle Avenues is indicative of a prosperous shopping street, which Jackson Avenue was into the early 1960s. Today mere survivorship there is an accomplishment. This building still stands, absent its dome and pediment over the second-story bay window. The southwest corner is a vacant lot. (Collection of Cynthia Harris.)

The Shingle Style, which was predominant in New Jersey architecture for much of the 1880s and 1890s, had an appealing interpretation for the urban store and apartment at an unknown corner on Ocean Avenue, a street where few frame structures survive. The card shows Tafts Pharmacy Number 227. (Collection of Cynthia Harris.)

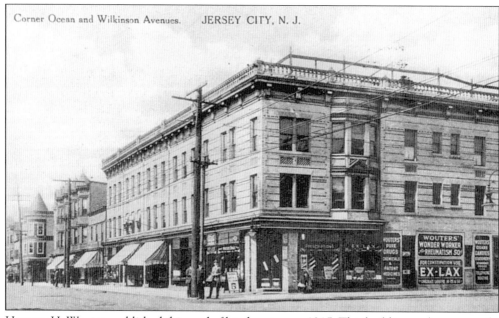

Herman H. Wouters published this card of his drugstore *c.* 1915. This building no longer stands. (Collection of Cynthia Harris.)

Observing street activity as a traditional urban pastime is reflected in the number of bay, bowed, and angled windows built in late-19th-century Jersey City buildings on busy avenues. The sender, frustrated by the inability to spoil the card with the traditional "x" had to resort to an arrow. Fred T. Hoele published the card *c.* 1912. (Collection of Cynthia Harris.)

Perhaps one advantage to the grocer of the ugly window signs announcing specials is their precluding the necessity of elaborate merchandise displays. How about the promotional slogan, "Fill your plate at Plate's," no? That is why the author writes history and not advertising copy. The store, seen on a *c.* 1912 card, is gone. (Collection of Cynthia Harris.)

The ice cream parlor is a vanishing fixture of the townscape. Its memory includes leather booths, counter stools, terrazzo floors, and a pleasant bouquet that was constant from one to the other. The author has long-wondered exactly what ingredients created the inimitable fragrance; they no doubt included chocolate and malt, but what else? The entrance at right is recognizable today, but the gated storefront shuts out the memories. (Collection of Cynthia Harris.)

The Romanesque Revival was a favored style in the 1890s to reflect solidity and substance in bank structures. The Greenville Banking and Trust Company is seen c. 1915 in Henry Lembeck's office building on the southeast corner. He was a substantial property owner, as well as brewer of the well-known Lembeck & Betz beer. (Collection of Cynthia Harris.)

Incredible is the word for the survival of Gotthardt's small florist shop, especially in an area with so many structural casualties. Seen *c.* 1910, it still stands at 311 Ocean Avenue, with the front altered and the greenhouse bricked in. Notice his sign. If one wishes to enter that line today, there is plenty of prospective business in the nearby overgrown cemeteries. (Collection of Cynthia Harris.)

Dolbear's former show store still stands at 120 Ocean Avenue. The front is gated and the building is missing its decorative finish. (Collection of Cynthia Harris.)

Perhaps that child did not understand that "Don't play in the street" also meant not waiting there for photographers. (Collection of Cynthia Harris.)

This c. 1908 view of Rutgers Street appears to be northwesterly, from the roof of P.S. 20. (Collection of Cynthia Harris.)

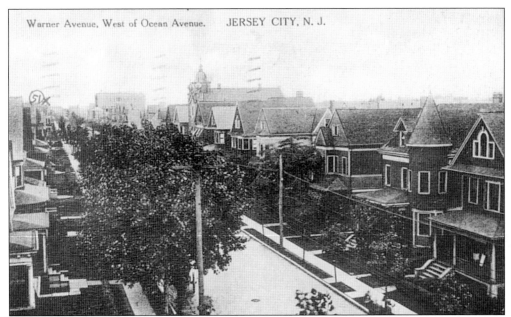

This view of Warner was taken c. 1910, a short distance west of Ocean Avenue (a corner where an abandoned cemetery monument yard seems to have some good bargains). Number 24, with the tower, and number 26 (adjacent) stand, but a brick house replaced the next one on a largely stable street. (Collection of Cynthia Harris.)

Danforth Ave.,
JERSEY CITY, N. J.

Danforth Avenue, a wide, tree-lined thoroughfare, runs virtually the entire width of Greenville. It is appealingly reflected in this c. 1908 Perlenfein card. (Collection of Cynthia Harris.)

St. Paul's Roman Catholic Church, founded by the Passionist Fathers of West Hoboken in 1861, was first housed in a small frame church built in 1862. It was located on Old Bergen Road, between Greenville and Linden Avenues. The pictured Gothic Revival edifice, their second, which stands at the northwest corner of Old Bergen Road and Greenville Avenue, was built in 1887–88, with Bishop Wigger present for the cornerstone laying on May 29, 1887, and the dedication July 15, 1888. The church is well-preserved and little-changed. The former school, seen behind the church in this *c.* 1910 card, was built *c.* 1890 and replaced by the 1926 structure at Old Bergen Road and Lembeck Avenue. (Collection of Cynthia Harris.)

William Buchbinder's pharmacy, located at 239 Old Bergen Road, is distinctive with its fixed, framed canopy. The building still stands, absent the canopy, at Danforth Avenue. Buchbinders published the card *c.* 1904. (Collection of Cynthia Harris.)

St. Paul's is seen *c.* 1910 in its street context, looking north from Lembeck Avenue, the site (at left) of its present school. St. Ann's Home is located on the lot behind the fence at right; its older part is in the former Lembeck residence. (Collection of Cynthia Harris.)

The major intersection of Old Bergen Road and Danforth Avenue is well represented in postcard views; this example was published by Buchbinder, a store seen at right, *c.* 1910. The view is looking south towards St. Paul's. The commercial building seen at left is no longer extant. (Collection of Cynthia Harris.)

Garfield Ave., Greenville, Jersey City, N. J.

The origin of Garfield Avenue was the former Bergen Point Plank Road, a Greenville thoroughfare to southern Bayonne that was once lined with large houses on spacious grounds. The older character has been removed totally, making it nearly impossible to identify corners such as the one on the c. 1910 Voigt No. 256. (Collection of Cynthia Harris.)

Raymund Roth Pioneer Home. Greenville, Jersey City, N. J.

The Raymond Roth Pioneer Home, founded in 1887, was located at 574 Garfield Avenue, opposite Dwight Street, on a lot backing up to the Central Railroad tracks. Roth had a downtown insurance business. The appealing, c. 1880s Shingle-style structure housed a German home for U.S. citizens over age 65. The organization was merged into the Fritz Reuter Altenheim at an unspecified date, while the building pictured on c. 1910 Voigt No. 258 was demolished c. 1960. (Collection of Cynthia Harris.)

Arlington Avenue still looks much like it did *c.* 1910, as seen on this Voigt No. 264. A nice Colonial Revival house at right, number 154, is marred by its brickface on the porch. The gambrel-roofed, number 160 next to it is recognizable, while another house fills part of the lot between the two. (Collection of Cynthia Harris.)

This Claremont Avenue scene, *c.* 1910, appears to be looking east toward Jackson Avenue (Martin Luther King Drive), a judgment made believing the building at left is number 190. If so, its twin is gone, while there are few other reliable identification hints present now.

The early-18th-century Hancock house, which once stood at the foot of Chapel Avenue near the bay, is seen in the context of its surroundings, east of the Lehigh Valley tracks and the Morris Canal and south of Cavan Point. The house, seen here in a c. 1910 view, was visited by Lafayette, according to local lore. It disappeared at an unknown date. The inset shows the east facade. (Courtesy of John Rhody.)

Black Tom, a former island in New York Bay that over time became attached to the Jersey City mainland east of Cavan Point, was the site of a munitions loading pier that was shipping arms to the Allies during World War I. A series of massive explosions shook the city in the early morning hours on Sunday, July 30, 1916, causing extensive damage in Hudson County's worst-ever disaster. About five lives were lost. The destruction was long-thought to be the work of German saboteurs, a belief that was not revealed conclusively until 1953. The exact site of the pictured damage scene is not identified. (Collection of Cynthia Harris.)

Van Nostrand Ave. C. R. R. Station, JERSEY CITY, N. J.

The main line of the Central Railroad was located between Garfield Avenue and the Morris Canal in southern Greenville. The Van Nostrand station, seen on a c. 1910 card issued by Perlenfein Brothers, another publisher of an extended Jersey City series, was located at the foot of Van Nostrand Avenue at Bay Side Park. The Pioneer Home, seen on page 120, is visible at right. One of the larger, but later houses that once lined Garfield Avenue, is at left. (Collection of Cynthia Harris.)

Greenville Car Station Ocean Ave. Greenville N. J.

This station may have been the one on the west side of Ocean Avenue, at the corner of Gates. An obscured destination marker also mars identification, but the Greenville Line had a Gates Avenue stop before proceeding to Bayonne. (Collection of Cynthia Harris.)

The Boulevard bridge over the Morris Canal on the Jersey City-Bayonne border was the center of a pastoral scene when photographed c. 1905 by Charles Lefferts. It is an example of interest in a picture for what it does not show—later development. (Collection Jersey City Public Library.)

Curries Woods, fixed in memory for the 1959 housing project, was part of an extensive farm on both the Greenville and Bayonne sides of the border. It was owned by Scotland native James Currie, who was born 1800 and was a c. 1840 emigrant to the United States. The precise spot on this c. 1908 Perlenfein Brothers card is not identified, but is perhaps near the place where Currie and his wife Ellen had 11 children. Only a handful of farmers remained in Hudson County by 1910. (Collection of Cynthia Harris.)

Eight

HUMAN INTEREST

The original version of this 1907 photographic card is marked "Waiting for the paymaster D.L.&W. RR" (Delaware Lackawanna & Western). From their looks, it would be advisable that the paymaster should not be late. If he did not appear at all, the preferable course of action would have been taking the nearest long-distance train, preferably the Pennsylvania, as that line west farther west than the D.L.&W. (Collection of Cynthia Harris.)

This page's two pictures address the question of what makes a postcard. Frances Kelly's promotion of war savings stamps has been found in a number of collections. The cards are unmarked and without a postcard "back," (a vertical line dividing the address side of the card and the slogan "post card"). However, the makeup of the card makes it appear a near certainty that it was manufactured for the mail, the absence of a postcard "back" notwithstanding. However, purists wonder. (Collection of Gary Dubnik.)

Katherine Higgins alighted from a Montgomery Street trolley on September 29, 1907, stepped in front of another on an adjoining track, was struck, and lost a leg from her injuries. A man named Julius, perhaps a passer-by, photographed the scene and had his picture printed on postcard stock. Thus, his snapshot is a legitimate "real photograph" post card, to use the popular, but redundant, term. Commercial photographers made a business of printing such photographic cards, such as Charles Lefferts, whose work is illustrated liberally throughout, but anyone with the right paper could make a photographic postcard. (Courtesy of John Rhody.)

This *c.* 1940s photographic postcard of a Jersey City International League pitcher was probably made for response to his fan mail. This unused example regrettably did not include his name. Experience has taught one of the best ways to have a picture identified is to publish it in anonymity. (Collection of Harold Solomon.)

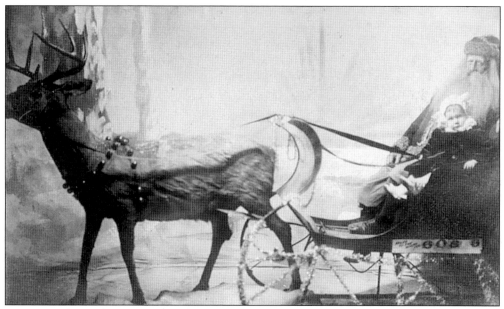

One concedes working as Santa Claus is not easy, nor is it likely a simple matter to find good ones. However, the first person to view this *c.* 1915 card said Santa looked sinister! His youthful companion, Nicholas (no relation to the saint) Frank Woolley (known as Frank), lives in retirement at the shore.

Carlo, your card says it all, making a caption almost redundant. This example was mailed in 1935 to confirm a gig at Stuart McNamara's New York City residence, demonstrating that his entertainment crossed ethnic as well as state lines. Restivo seemed so versatile that if he left his instrument in a taxi, one imagines he could have made hand-clapping percussion music (which may have sounded better than the accordion). (Courtesy of John Rhody.)

The Nathan Rapaport sculpture *Liberation*, an American soldier carrying a WW II concentration camp survivor, was dedicated in 1985 in Liberty State Park as a Holocaust Memorial. The background is also of major interest, the Jersey Cityite's view of the Statue of Liberty. The Frederic-Auguste Bartholdi statue, on the Richard Morris Hunt-designed base on Liberty Island, would have been in Jersey City water if not for a bi-state pact that granted the island to the State of New York. Note the partial scaffolding, which eventually enveloped the statue. It was erected for the 1984–86 restoration and repair project for its 1986 centennial.